# HOPE REMAINS:

## *The Audacity of Faith*

### A MEMOIR

# BY SAMANTHA N. WHITE

Hope Remains: The Audacity of Faith (A Memoir)

White, Samantha N.

978-1-3999-7360-1    Paperback
978-1-3999-7361-8    eBook

Book Production by Dawn James, Publish and Promote
Editor Christine Bode, Bodacious Copy
Cover design by Publish and Promote
Interior design and layout by Perseus Design

Printed and bound in the United Kingdom.

**Note to the reader:**
The events in this book are based on the author's memories from her perspective. Certain names have been changed to protect the identities of those mentioned. Any similarity to real persons, places, incidents, or actions is coincidental. The information is provided for educational and inspirational purposes only.

# CONTENTS

# REDIRECTION

# THE FALL

G liding through dense canopies of vibrant trees, I am greeted by a familiar landscape on this momentous day. As this vehicle dominates the curvature and variances of the road, its splendour unveils centuries of pride and history. The vehicle advances effortlessly to our destination as these buildings proudly stand, dancing gloriously in the warmth of the sun.

Tears roll down my cheek as I look around in a trance, reflecting on the months of turmoil—internal and external—that I have had to overcome to arrive at this juncture. How did I arrive here? Only by the grace of God. I settle before easing back into my seat whilst twitching my sandals anxiously.

As the car pulls to a halt in the delegated car park, gratitude engulfs me. I whisper a prayer and say under my breath, *well done.*

Checking the time, I realise I have fifteen minutes to be robed and seated in the hall before the event begins: Graduation 2022. Two years late, but it is better to be delayed than cancelled altogether.

Walking briskly to the venue's location, I am determined to be on time. Catching sight of an attendee, I head towards her with a dogged focus to enquire about the venue's location. In amazement, she points in that direction. Thanking her, I instruct my guests on how to find their way to the venue. Then suddenly, I take off like Bolt in a 100-metre track and field race.

Dust rises as my feet pound the gravelled path.

*This is stupid!* I hiss my teeth in frustration, sigh, and then immediately kneel to the ground. Nothing will stop me from being on time. So, I unbuckle my nude five-inch platform heels and sprint with complete conviction along the path while holding onto them like my life depends on them.

*I don't care how crazy I look! Nothing will hinder me.* One by one, each foot begins to pound the ground—the same way I have been running towards my destiny.

A sharp pain shoots up the soles of my feet, so to mitigate it, I seek temporary refuge on the adjacent grassed lawn while I keep running.

Dust and gravel flying, the sun peers down intently like my own spotlight—challenging and cheering me on simultaneously.

'Almost there!' I say, motivating my efforts. As the building draws near, my journey to this point flashes across my eyes: I was ripping up the narrative of reoccurring generational behaviours that have stifled the growth of my family's bloodline.

One final hurdle, I think as I briskly launch one foot ahead of the other.

'I'm alllmmost…thherre!!' I shout as I find myself falling face-first on the provisionally constructed path.

If you are wondering how I arrived here, my story is one filled with challenges, cliffhangers, and crossroads. Had I not gone through it, I would have believed it was fictional. Still intrigued? Continue reading, and I will reveal some pivotal events that have brought me to this moment.

## The Journey
***

Over seven years ago, in January 2016, to be exact, I was knee-deep in paperwork. It was month-end, the last week in January, and I had reached breaking point. Month after month, at month-end, I had been arriving at the office at 08:00 a.m. and leaving around 22:30 p.m.

'There must be another way!' I groaned while sinking my teeth into a pencil.

This process was time-consuming, and wasting almost forty-eight hours sifting through hundreds of pages was not an efficient use of my time.

Instead of the accounting software unsystematically sending clients' paperwork directly to the printer, it could skip that stage and send the documents to a folder on my computer's desktop.

'Jonathan, I have an idea of how to speed up our month-end processes. Look, here is a little sketch of the entire process, both current and with my tweaks. Is this feasible?'

'Let's have a look. Uuummhh…OK. So, are you saying if these steps are removed and replaced with this one new step, we would have a faster process?'

'Yes, exactly! Does it make sense?' I anxiously asked while staring at Jonathan's intrigued disposition.

Jonathan was Australian, and he was backpacking across Europe with his girlfriend. He was working as an interim finance manager who, not surprisingly, embodied the idea of how one would stereotypically describe an Aussie. He always looked relaxed and was never nervous but looked like he had just finished surfing due to his sporting dishevelled clothes. In contrast, he was quite good at his job, and somehow, his laissez-faire nature made you lean in for more.

'So, what do I do now? Should I pitch this new process to Pat?'

'Why not? It's a brilliant idea! There is no way that he can reject it. Sell it to him. What are the benefits of incorporating this new system? Lead with the advances, and he will have to at least give your idea a good thought.'

'Thanks a lot, Jonathan! I am going to go for it.'

'Well done, Sam and good luck!'

With an extra boost of confidence, I returned to my desk while rehearsing how I would pitch the new system idea to Pat.

Approximately three minutes to 12:15 p.m., the meeting between Pat and Gary ended. I watched patiently as Pat returned to his desk. He logged onto his desktop and then immediately made his way to the kitchen with his coffee mug in hand.

*OK, Sam. This is your chance; it's GO time!* I said to myself as Pat emerged from the kitchen a few minutes later and headed towards his desk whilst sipping slowly from his mug.

'Pat! May I have a few minutes of your time?'

'Sure, how can I help?'

'As you know, month-end just wrapped up. You may not be aware, but I have been feeling overwhelmed with the amount of work I had to do during the week that led to it.'

'I was not aware of this. Why didn't you raise your concerns with me?'

'I didn't want to cause a fuss.'

'For some time now, I have been coming in at 08:00 a.m. and leaving at around 22:00 p.m. on the last week of every month for over six months to ensure I get our clients' accounts up-to-date before the accountants run month-end reports.'

'You should have told us so that we could have compensated you with food and travel', said Pat frustratedly.

'No one told me that was a possibility! Besides, would I get compensated now for the many months that have passed?'

'No, too much time has lapsed', Pat stated regrettably while itching the crown of his head, then fixing his hair back into position with an effortless flick of his left hand.

'Oh well, it's OK. So, I requested your time to let you know that I have designed a new process that I feel will eliminate the backlog I have been facing, which could speed up my phase. Please look!' I said while passing my sketches to him.

After a few minutes of analysing them, Pat said, 'It looks good; however, we don't have the budget for a new system. So, if it is going to cost the company money, it will have to be a no.'

'It will not. It is straightforward and should not take up many resources', I said reassuringly.

'Right! I will locate an IT manager who can help you with it. Leave it with me. I will speak with someone in IT to get them to help you, and just remember, if it's going to need money to be realised, it will be terminated.'

'It shouldn't!' I confirmed dubiously.

There will be times when your brilliant and effective ideas will be shot down. Please do not accept it as a sign to not voice your future opinions or inputs. There are several factors at play—known and unknown. On earlier occasions, when my ideas were dismissed, it was out of fear—the Treasury manager had a tight budget, and he wanted to keep all expenses within that target.

**However, growth is impossible without challenge.**

In the Book of James, God encourages us to be joyful when we face trials because our faith is being tested, which will produce patience. Challenges are inevitable, so when you are going through them, it can be overwhelming. In my experience, I have had to reflect on how I have grown from each trial so that I could be encouraged for the next challenge.

---

*"My brethren, count it all joy when you fall into various trials, knowing that the testing of your faith produces patience." James 1:2-3*

---

# BURNOUT

'I am knackered!' I shrieked.

It had been nonstop all day. I was exhausted, and I didn't think I could finish my shift. I grimaced. My waistline was aching, and my fingers were frozen frankfurters. I had been kneeling on a tattered mat on the bottom shelf of the aisle for the last twenty-one minutes and counting.

'Another twelve-hour day!' I moaned while massaging my waist.

This night was tough. I had been operating on four hours of sleep, coffee, and illegal amounts of sugar and failing miserably. I was running on overdrive.

'My poor heart!'

'Pardon?' said a male patron.

'Oh! My apologies, I was simply thinking out loud.'

With a blank stare, he slowly nodded, smiled, and advanced along the aisle.

'I need another job!' I concluded as I continued unloading the box of frozen products.

'Sam!' hollered Tracy.

'Yes!' I answered as I walked towards her voice, bellowing over the tops of groceries. Wandering to the end of the aisle and taking a right turn, I came face to face with her.

'Hey, Tracy! You called?'

Tracy was the night-shift manager for Rootes Grocery Store. She had been my confidante, counsellor, and sounding board for the past three months.

Standing at 160 centimetres and 50 kilograms soaking wet, Tracy was petite, sporting her signature bountiful head of curls that directly contrasted with her pale porcelain skin. Biracial with a White Scottish father and a Black Caribbean mother, she was the embodiment of light in a dark room.

'I'm arranging everyone's break. What time do you need your break?'

'What time is it now?'

'19:49.'

'I'll take my break at 21:00 if it is available.'

'Yes, that time is still available. What are you working on currently?'

'I'm replenishing frozen stocks. I have three small boxes left.'

'Brilliant! Once you are through with the frozen stock, you can move to water, then soft drinks.'

'OK, will do, though my head feels heavy', I informed Tracy as intense pain crept up the back of my neck from my depleted shoulder blades.

'Take your break now, Sam. It has been a hectic day', said Tracy. 'Do you have a headache? I have painkillers if you need them.'

'I am going to purchase one of those chicken burgers and make a cup of tea. I'll wait to see how I feel after, and if my head is still throbbing in fifteen minutes, I will come to find you for the painkillers.'

Since September 2017, I have been a constant fixture at this store. The following week would be the second week of December, and every morning, I rolled out of bed with aches and pain from burning the midnight oil at both ends. I was exhausted mentally and physically, but I had no other option. I had to finish what I had started.

I couldn't believe I'd worked in that role for so long. It had been a steep uphill climb. I was struggling to do it, but I refused to quit. I couldn't afford to quit. The only way I could push through daily was by holding steadfast to what I knew. *It would work out for my good.* That was as much as my mind could take; I couldn't take any more.

The last two weeks had been particularly draining. Last Thursday night at approximately 22:50 p.m., after finishing my shift as a cleaner at the hospital, I learnt that I had failed my Strategy exam. This module was a core topic for my degree—Master's in Business with Consulting at my university—Warwick Business School. That realisation had me in a daze of disbelief, with several thoughts dancing around my mind and adding to the weight of worry trying to shackle me to my current position. With tears pouring down my cheeks, I weighed my options because I felt stuck between a rock and a hard place. At that moment, I was too tired to think of how to navigate myself out of that predicament.

'Sam, what's wrong?' asked Fatima, the night shift supervisor.

Fatima is statuesque. Standing at 173 centimetres and 83 kilograms, her plum rosy cheeks protruded around her tightly wound dark brown hijab that complimented her straight black hair and dark brown eyes.

'I am overwhelmed, Fatima. I came here to obtain my degree, but I am working every waking moment, which is detracting from my studies, to pay my bills—accommodation, my studies, and necessities. I don't know what to do. Moreover, the loan that I was depending on fell through, and with my status in this country being only an Indefinite Leave to Remain, I am unable to secure a postgraduate loan to cover my expenses. I don't have family members I can secure aid from; we are all in the same boat—we must help each other.'

'I empathise with you, Sam. In the past, I wanted support from my family to continue my education, and my father flat-out declined. He said it would be a waste of time and money because I was going to be someone's wife, so he wouldn't get a return on his investment.' Fatima's eyes filled with tears.

'I am so sorry to hear. Did you try to undertake your studies on your own?'

'I tried, then my father found out and told me that if I wanted to pursue a career, I would have to do it under my own roof. The worst thing is that he sent both of my brothers to the best schools. One's a doctor—a general practitioner—and the other is an engineer. All I wanted was to go to nursing school. I was angry for years, and I made a promise to myself. I told my husband before we got married that if we have girls, they will be educated at the same level as their brothers, no matter what. If I had a higher level of education, I could have been more than a supervisor in a supermarket.'

'Wow! I am truly sorry to hear of your struggles. We always think the grass is greener, but I guess all families have their own trials. I am in this predicament because I want better for myself, my family, and my future children. I have gone through so much, but I cannot give up. I gave up everything to return to university on the instruction of God.'

'I see. Where are your parents?' said Fatima as she pulled up a chair to the table where I was seated.

'It is a long story, but my parents are in the Caribbean—Jamaica—to be exact. My journey to this point has been tumultuous and complicated. I have been homeless since I was sixteen years old. My mother only has me, and I do not have any family in the UK. Bear with me, and I will quickly bring you up to date.'

'For the last three months, Friday nights have conjured up a feeling of distress and unease.'

'Why?' probed Fatima.

'Because every Friday night, I am stranded on campus with no way of travelling to my accommodation, which is approximately ten miles from campus and requires two buses. With the last bus leaving campus at 23:00 p.m., which coincides with the end of my shift, even if I leave work five minutes early, by the time I arrive at the bus terminus in town to board the second bus, I get stranded there, because the bus has already left which is extremely unsafe. So, for the last three months and one week, I have been unable to rest my head in a warm bed for two nights out of a week. Therefore, as I could not leave campus, I was forced to stay in the university's library, which is open twenty-four hours.

'That can't be healthy, Sam', said Fatima.

'I have no other option, Fatima. At least the library is open, so I have somewhere clean, dry, and warm to stay during the night. Although the library has a no sleeping policy, I adhere to this by trying my hardest to stay awake by washing my face hourly, but I keep dozing off. To pass the time, I try to incorporate extra reading to keep up with my studies, as most of my spare time is filled with work.

'Sadly, the limited amount of sleep is taxing on my body, and I've been consuming large quantities of sugary products and strong, bitter coffee, but this hasn't been entirely effective as of late. This concoction of fuel is not sustaining the efficient functioning of my body, and I've been experiencing sharp stomach aches, tightened chest, and shivers. With all that said, I have been striving to push through each day by the grace of God.'

'Insha'Allah! Have you spoken to anyone in your department about getting a room on campus?' said Fatima.

'No. Back in September, during the induction week, I was informed that all campus accommodations were filled. I was lucky to secure a place. I'm staying at my aunt's friend's property on the other side of the city—ten miles away—hence needing two buses to get there.

'It has been a struggle, and last night, Friday, was one of my worst nights yet. It was extremely challenging. I couldn't focus, and trying to stay awake was the furthest thing from my mind. I dozed off numerous times, and every time I did, a security guard tapped me on my shoulders to wake up. A combination of strolling back and forth and the frequent splashing of water onto my face kept me awake, but only for a short time. On an hourly basis, I revisited the toilet to splash cold water onto my face. Bloodshot eyes and a swollen face reflected back as I stared in the mirror. I placed my face into the palms of my hands.

'*God, I can't do this!*' I said. My entire body ached. All I needed was to close my eyes for a few minutes. 'I'm not doing this anymore!'

'*Nothing is working!*' I moaned as I massaged my forehead. The crash was coming, and there was nothing that I could do to halt it.

'So, with total conviction, I walked back to the desk where I was positioned. I quickly glanced around to check whether the security guard could see me. Unable to locate him, I hastily packed my rucksack and returned to the female toilet.

'Returning to the toilet, I was a dog with a bone. I checked that all six stalls—three on the left and right—were cleared while assessing which was positioned in the right location to try to get a quick nap without getting caught. Once cleared, I tried the stall on the right, closest to the mirrors, but then declined because it would be readily accessible and visible. So, walking diagonally, I went to the stall on the far left—at the extreme corner—out of sight—but too much light was catching it, so if someone were to use the toilet, I would be quickly awoken. With that revelation, I declined and moved immediately opposite—on the right—to the stall with the least visibility.

'At that moment, I was shaking feverishly; sleep had arrived. It crashed down on me like a mighty wave smashing against a shore, and I had lost all control over my body—I needed to sleep. I precariously stacked my rucksack on the toilet holder, and with my scarf, I covered my head and shoulder, and almost instantaneously, I was out for the count.'

'Sam, that cannot be good. You slept in the stalls of the university library's toilet last night? OMG! You must feel like hell. How are you managing to stay awake?' Fatima said, concerned.

'It's been a long day. I'm on my third cup of coffee. I've had two energy drinks and a bag of sweets. I am exhausted and don't know what I will do tonight. I'm aching and desperately need somewhere to lay down.'

'Sam! Your break is up', said Tracy as she entered the breakroom.

'Tracy, have you heard where Sam slept last night?' asked Fatima.

'No, I haven't, where? Where did you sleep last night?' said Tracy, staring at me.

'Well, I slept in the library's toilet. I think I slept for around four hours. It was uncomfortable, but there was no other option.'

'Poor you. Sam, would you mind leaving thirty minutes early? It has calmed down now, and there are three of us, so we can cope so that you can get some proper rest tonight. Try to make it home and get some rest. You can start thirty minutes early tomorrow to make up for your hours. Actually, you can go now. It's 10:34 p.m.', insisted Tracy.

'You sure? Thank you so much, Tracy!' I squealed while jumping to my feet swiftly, gathering my things.

*I am not going to change out of my work clothes. I don't want to miss the last bus.*

Checking the time, I realised I had five minutes to get to the bus stop.

'Good night, all! Those of you who are working tomorrow, see you then; if not, have a good weekend. See you soon. Bye, I gotta go!' I said as I rushed through the door.

Turning right and walking briskly towards the bus stop, I saw the last bus to the city centre. *Yes, thank you, Lord!* Holding my rucksack securely to my back, I increased my speed.

The bus lit up. I could see the driver starting the engine. Then, the bus began to slowly move off.

'NO! Wait!! I'm here, please stop!' I shout while running towards the moving bus. 'No!!' I scream desperately.

*I just want a warm bed tonight. What am I going to do?*

Defeated, I grabbed my shoes while dragging my rucksack in my left hand.

*Lord, I need a bed tonight. I can't spend another night in the library's toilet. Please make a way,* I pleaded as I wandered towards the library.

While doing so, a thought came to me. *Check if you have access to your Business School.* My department's building is on the opposite side of the road (the left-hand side) to the library. Clinging to that idea, I crossed the street and aimed for the grand bespoke building that stands in stark contrast to the ancient library. Rummaging around in my bag, I located my ID card. Holding my breath, I scanned my ID card and closed my eyes, praying...*please open, please*!

Click—the sound of the latch unlocking caused my heart to race. I pulled the door towards me. 'It's open? It's OPEN!!' I shouted with tears streaming down my cheeks.

After dancing around ecstatically, I consoled myself.

Nervously, I walked through the door while scanning the hall to see if anyone was in the building. *Empty, no one?!*

I sauntered to the student lounge on the third floor, holding my breath once more while scanning my ID card at its entrance. Again, the door opened. Moseying into the lounge, I was elated. With immense delight, I nose-dived onto the largest sofa.

Opening a sweet and salty popcorn, I snuggled under my scarf and jacket, then scanned my laptop for a movie. As the movie commenced, the memory of failing my exam came rushing back like streaming water from a broken pipe, stealing my moment of bliss.

Reflecting on receiving my grades, my chest tightened, and anxiety jerked me sober. Drowning, an overwhelming number of emotions convicted me. In the blink of an eye, I was halfway down a page, consructing a letter seeking deferral.

*The Email*

Good morning, Mr Rob,

I need your help, please!

My time on this course has been incredibly trying, with the SFE (Student Finance England) company's inability to offer me the Postgraduate Loan, which I have been fighting since August 2017, and scouring the internet for other loan offers to no avail.

This feeling of helplessness and frustration came to a head on the 7th of December at 04:30 a.m. when the desire to end it all rose inside me. Where I stay, a brook is close, and all I wanted to do was to walk into it. As I write, my eyes tear up. I am emotionally and physically drained, fighting with every fibre of my being to get this opportunity to study at this prestigious establishment. Since October, I have been sleeping on campus in the library and by the grace of God, I stumbled into the postgraduate PG Hub because I have no other option—having a shift that ends at 23:15 p.m. and sometimes another at 12:00 midnight means that I am stuck here as I currently stay in Little Heath and the last bus that leaves from Pool Meadow Station is at 23:00 p.m.

My journey to date has been excruciatingly difficult. Coupled with what I mentioned above, I am being chased for payment from the Credit Control team and last week, I was sent another outstanding request to pay the remaining balance of my tuition by March. I simply can't find this money, and they said that if I cannot do so, they will suspend my studies...

Once your goal or purpose has been established, do not waver. Writing your vision and making it plain is not simply for display and inspiration. It is for the challenging days when every fibre in your body tells you to do everything but work on bringing your goals to fruition. It is for those lonely days and cold nights when you are awake working on your vision at stupid o'clock (00:00 – 05:00 a.m.) when the world seems to be sleeping. You remain steadfast and look at your visions at moments of weakness.

Also, I have discovered that if you do not break the trials you face, your children will deal with the same issues. So, if not you, then who? Your offspring?

***Trust the process.***

Corinthians reminds us that God has given us *grace* to overcome our hurdles and setbacks because in our weakness, He is strong, but we need to trust the route that He takes us along to shatter these hurdles.

---

*"My grace is sufficient for you, for my power is made perfect in weakness."*
*2 Corinthians 12:9-10*

---

# POSSIBILITIES

*A larm bellowing!!*

Jolted from my sleep—disoriented—the surroundings were unfamiliar for a few seconds. It was an unrecognisable space. Moments later, reality punched me in the stomach, and all the memories from the previous night came rushing back, disguising a sharp pain that exploded across my frontal lobe, feeling like I was fighting in my sleep. With my eyes wide open, I felt as though something had hit me on my head.

The alarm bellowed even louder, and this time, I started searching for it. Cushions were all on the floor—nothing. Checked under the sofa; still nothing. 'Where is it?!' I blurted out frustratedly.

The phone's alarm went off once more but with even more power.

Focusing on the vibration, I was able to locate my phone. It was trapped down the back of the sofa, exactly where I slept. It could have been forced through some loose threads that unravelled. Once I identified the entry point, I could manoeuvre the phone to the breached fabric and pull it through.

Checking the time, I saw it was 05:34 a.m. My eyes opened wide, darting around sceptically.

For a few seconds, I was a disoriented floating log, heavy and numb. Nothing was recognisable. Instantly, the memories of what transpired the night before flooded my memory like an ice avalanche cascading down a smooth mountain the night after a snowstorm.

Manically, I rummaged around for my laptop. Its battery died in the early morning, so I plugged it in while I waited for its reboot. With beads of regret, I scanned my emails and checked my Sent box. Nothing. *I swore I wrote a letter questioning the possibility of deferring my studies.*

'I was certain of it', I murmured to myself.

'What? What's going on? Where is my message?!'

*Wait, what happened last night? Did I delete it accidentally, or did I send it?*

After exhausting all possibilities, I found my email suspended in the Outbox. I double-clicked on it to open the message, and it disappeared.

'Oh no! What have I done?'

Opening the Sent folder, there it is, sent.

I sent an incomplete deferral request email to the head of my degree coordinator.

# POSSIBILITIES

*What am I going to do?*

I could do nothing as it was Sunday, so I shut down my laptop.

Feeling defeatist, I nervously wandered around the building. On my journey to the ground floor, I remembered one of the lecturers saying that they cycled to work and showered in one of the designated showers. So, with this knowledge, I continued searching for it. Hidden behind students' lockers on the left-hand side of the hallway was a maroon fire door.

I pushed open the heavy fire door to access the shower rooms. Behind it were four showers, one labelled 'Disabled.' Using the shower without authority was an unnerving experience. As such, the entire process took a little under fifteen minutes. I focused on not getting caught and completed the fastest shower ever.

Journeying from the shower rooms back to where I had slept the night before was comparable to a truly awful scene from an early 2000s spy movie that got excluded on the editing floor.

Managing to escape the attention of the few early risers who roamed the building, I was safely back in the confines of the student lounge. Perching on the sofa, I decided to unwind as I had time before commencing my shift, so I threw my scarf over my face. My mind raced. I began reflecting on the challenges I overcame that led me to that place. While reflecting, I dozed off...

## First Prison Visit
***

As I woke, I was in the middle of a journey.

It was a beautiful autumn day, and the sea of trees in full splendour layered with an astounding house of leaves perfectly positioned to be sun-kissed. As the bus glided along its route towards High Down, I sat in awe of the scenery. Had this moment not been affected by the weight of my first prison visit, I could have enjoyed the vibrant leaves on full display.

'We are now approaching the final destination: HMP High Down', confirmed a reassuring feminine voice as it escaped from the bus speakers and punctured the thick cloud of worry weighing passengers' countenances.

As bus No. 8 gently approaches its destination, a small cottage-size outbuilding is situated on the side of the prison's compound. Positioned on the left, the sight of the prison's structure dumbfounded me. I glanced around and noticed that I was all alone. All the other visitors were comprised of two to three individuals—people to carry and distribute their burdens of sadness.

Immediately, loneliness crept up and cloaked me, and to mask my disappointment, I peered down at my profile picture on my travel card. Simultaneously, I gripped it tightly to simulate comfort and reassurance by my loved ones. As I waited for the other passengers to progress forward for us to disembark the bus, I closed my eyes, wishing that I was hugging my grandmother.

'Miss, miss, miss!' called the bus driver.

I opened my eyes and stared at the man yelling at me with confusion.

'Please take your things and leave the bus. You're the last passenger left. Are you getting off here or continuing the journey back to Sutton City Centre?'

'Yes, I am getting off here', I said nervously while displaying an awkward smile. I collected all my things and promptly exited the bus.

Ushered to the reception in the outbuilding, we were instructed to display our IDs, so I adhered to the request. I held up my travel card to the left side of my face for easy comparison. The officer glanced back and forth from the ID to my face, and then she ordered me to hand it to her for a closer inspection.

*Please, Lord, let her say yes!*

'This is all I have', I said candidly while intently observing the officer behind the Perspex screen examining details on my ID. 'I only have my travel card as proof of identity. I need access today. I came so far.' I prayed quickly with my eyes wide open.

So, there I was, waiting for this officer to view my travel card as my passport was tied up at the home office.

'Miss, here is your travel card. Now move along!' said an officer.

'She said move along', affirmed a visitor standing immediately behind me.

I smiled nervously. Thanked her. Then, I shuffled along the queue to retrieve a locker key to store my things.

Once we were all processed, we congregated in the seating area. The silence was deafening.

While anxiously awaiting further instructions, I started to think about how I would feel to be sentenced, but it was impossible as I did not have a reference point. While wrestling with that thought, we received directions to leave the building, so we formed a line and marched towards the entrance of the humungous, unassuming, natural-toned building outside.

Entering the building, I received commands to stand on an 'X' in the middle of a square and not to fidget. I adhered to the orders and stood on the spot. An officer with a huge black dog approached me, and my heart started racing immediately.

'Do not make any sudden movements!' said the dog handler as he approached me with the dog.

Fear-stricken, I stared straight ahead and kept my eyes locked on the head of another visitor standing in a spot ahead of me who had their person sniffed by this dog, now smelling the fingers on my hands. The feeling of his wet nose on my left thumb yanked me back to 2002 when I arrived at Heathrow airport and had to stand still in a queue while enormous drug-trained dogs walked by and sniffed us.

I took my pass and walked to the main seating area, where another officer directed me to take a seat at the table on the left at the far corner of the room, where I waited for my mother to convene with me around the table.

The room felt sterile and claustrophobic. Painted white, with a pop of colour in the far left-hand corner, was a small, tactile, and multicoloured play area for small children to remain entertained and occupied over the one-hour visit. Planted purposefully around the room, officers are located every two meters from each other, observing every interaction between prisoners and visitors. Gifts had to be sent through the post to family members and could not be given on visits. Hugging must take no longer than two to three minutes under the scrutiny of officers to prevent the exchange of illegal objects such as drugs or mobile phones.

Family hugging was encouraged five minutes before the end of the one-hour visit, and inmates were returned to confinement. My mother and I hugged, and just like that, she was gone.

We, visitors, sat around awkwardly staring at each other while this occurred, and the room's silence was punctuated with gut-wrenching screams and cries from children who did not understand why their parents were leaving. This occurrence left an impression on me, and at that point, I made a personal promise to stay on the straight and narrow and do my best to avoid this predicament of becoming a statistic or getting involved in situations that would warrant imprisonment.

Visitors could exit in a single-line queue once the last prisoner left the meeting area. The walk back to the holding building was long, heart-wrenching, and depressing. The re-occurring metaphorical dark cloud hung extra low on this day. I felt overwhelmed, like I'd lost the hold on my reality. How would I escape the mess I'd been thrown in? As I took my bag out of the locker, I started to reflect on how quickly my life had spiralled out of control.

'The bus is here!' said an officer.

I exerted a massive sigh, then closed the locker door and returned the key to the front desk.

I felt deflated as we slowly boarded the No. 8 bus back to Sutton Station. My A Levels had suffered due to the upheaval, the uncertainty of my immigration status, and my future. Sleeping on the sofa at my grandma's friend's house did not help, but at least it was better than sleeping on the streets, so I couldn't complain. I was determined to become something, to obtain a university degree if it killed me, so I had to re-sit my A Levels.

As the season changed, I had faith that better would come. Yes, I struggled to juggle all these variables. I was drowning. I felt overwhelmed, but what was the opposite of my situation? Give up? I simply could not. If any of my cousins were in my position, I would like to think they would fight for their future. Everything was up in the air.

One thing I knew was true: "I can do all things through Christ who strengthens me."

*How am I going to cope? What will happen to me?*

All I could do was keep the faith and continue attending church—my sanctuary—where I experienced some semblance of relief. That was all I could do for now, but I remained optimistic and would do my best to keep my promise to my grandmother—to make something of myself. There were several possibilities; I just needed to stay focused and tap into them. That thought brought tears to my eyes.

'Excuse me? Excuse me!' A series of taps on my shoulder jolted me awake. Did you sleep here all night?' a student asked.

'What if I did? Are you going to report me?'

'As long as you promise not to do it again', she replied.

'I'll try my best not to, but I can't make any promises', I said while putting my belongings into my rucksack. Checking the time, I realised that I had little under fifteen minutes to get to work, so I said goodbye and rushed out of the student lounge, down three flights of stairs, and turning left, I sprinted through the hallways, out the building and straight up the hill towards the supermarket.

Through my research, I learned that worrying is *faith* backwards. So, whenever a negative thought has you locked in uncertainty (a chokehold), remember past events with similar difficulty or stress levels and try your hardest to replay how you broke loose. Use that as the catalyst to remove negative thoughts from your mind that may be preventing you from tackling your next test.

***Remember: Celebrate the small wins! You got this! Just believe.***

Philippians informs us that we can do every good thing that comes as a gut feeling or a thought because these good ideas come from God, and he would not give them to you unless you are able to bring them to fruition. The idea to write and email a deferral letter came from God, so I knew that was the right thing to do.

---

*"I can do all things through Christ who strengthens me."*
*Philippians 4:13*

---

# A NEW CHAPTER

'Good morning, Charlie!'

'Morning, Sam!'

'Who is in today?' I asked as I rushed through the aisles, trying to get to the daily rota in the back office.

'What do you mean; which managers or supervisors?' said Charles, a native West Midlander widower in his late sixties who does this job because '...it is something to do...'

'Yes, my apology for the vagueness. Which supervisor or manager is working on the morning shift today?'

'Ah, OK. I believe it is Becky.'

'Yay! It's Becky. Right, thank you for that. I will say hello and ask her what she needs me to do.'

Rebecca 'Becky' Staine was an awesome supervisor. Another native West Midlander, she conjures hope and faith in humanity because she took a chance on me when

I was desperate and in need of a job upon moving here from London. I remember it as if it was yesterday...

**22:00 p.m., 21st September 2017**

A familiar and faithful face pulled up in a red rickety van.

'You're late!' I said.

'I'm sorry, Sam. Dale had to finish work and then come by my house to pick me up. I had to drive him back to his house before I came here', O'Shane explained.

My initial resistance waned with his apology sandwiched between a plausible apology and eagerness to transfer my clothing into the van.

Standing a little over 185 centimetres with an athletic build, O'Shane is a family friend I had become fond of. When I was going through the challenges with my mother being in prison, he was a sounding board that provided wisdom that helped me navigate the straight and narrow. Moreover, he helped me to remain motivated to hold onto the tiny light of hope at the end of a long, damp, and dreary tunnel.

Opening the back of his boot, O'Shane manoeuvred his friend's building tools to the right side of the van. Careening around the van, he went into further detail to explain what transpired while he waited for his friend to finish work and return.

'Where are your bags?' he asked, eyes darting around simultaneously.

'They are packed and sitting by the hallway.'

Forty-five minutes later, all my worldly possessions were squashed like sardines into this medium-sized van. Standing in the middle of my small, rented studio flat, I was overwhelmed yet hopeful. Was I nervous? Yes. I was anxious but mostly faithful because I had prayed for over a year for this opportunity. This new chapter should hopefully solidify me as an upstanding contributor to society.

'I am about to embark on this scary journey, Lord. Please order my steps and fight my battles as they arise', I whispered as I switched the lights off, closed, and locked the front door.

'Ready? Are you sure you have everything with you?' asked O'Shane.

'Yes, I have everything that I need. The only things I left behind were some groceries for Dean when he arrives', I confirmed soberly.

Almost fifty minutes later, O'Shane was coasting through Brent Cross on the A406 through the North Circular before merging with the M1 out of London. My next chapter was sealed.

As we edged closer to our destination, I was resolute in my decision. So, with newfound confidence, I opened my email to retrieve the login details I needed to check the result of the loan application I had applied for. Logging onto this webpage, I eagerly scanned the message for the answer: *"Unfortunately, at this time, we have decided to decline your application."*

Numb. I could not read any further. Nothing positive ever comes after this statement. I was sick to my stomach. I stared outside as the van whisked through Dunchurch.

'What did it say?' asked O'Shane.

'I was denied', I said abruptly.

*Lord, you told me that everything will be OK. I have turned my life upside down because of your instructions. Please intervene.* I pleaded.

### Three Months of Chaos
***

A little over three months ago, I was crammed into a church—Bright and Being Whole Gospel Church of God—completely submerged in the atmosphere of convention, which usually occurred during the last five days of August. This year, convocation was overflowing—more than usual and filled to the brim—the overflow room, aisles and every available section that could host a chair had someone placed there. Due to this, it was pertinent that I arrived early enough to snag a seat, especially as I came straight from work.

I was always lucky to secure a seat smack bang in the middle of the crowd in all locations of the church, left, right, and in the overflow room. That is where I felt most comfortable to be myself—sing as loud as I could—praise with the most verbosity and fortitude without feeling out of place. I was diligent; I made sure that once the clock struck 17:00 p.m., I was out of the office's door to ensure that I arrived at church at 18:00 p.m. on the hour.

*Consistency is better than sacrifice!* I reassured myself while selecting a seat on the left-hand side of the congregation, perfectly positioned in the middle.

Four days had lapsed, and nothing. I had been praying and fasting for two weeks prior to this convention, and nothing, no sign, no answer. Anxiously awaiting the church to be filled, I started to consider. *Today is the fifth and final day of convention. I am still awaiting a confirmation. I only have two weeks left. I need an answer, Lord. What should I do, Lord? Please give me an answer!* I murmured in my prayer.

'Please have a seat!' said the convention coordinator.

One minute later, a church member went to the rostrum to give their testimony, which was followed by a few more for fifteen minutes.

The congregation stood on the instruction of the choir director as the choir led us into praise. As the church erupted into praise and gratitude, the last key speaker proceeded to the pulpit. He joined in with the celebration for a few more minutes, followed by his greeting of the pastors, ministers, and congregation (saints).

As the noise settled and the preacher was embraced by convention attendees, Bishop Rogers took them through an emotional resurgence of hope and prosperity. While his message was being received, several members of the congregation were becoming animated arbitrarily with praise of admiration and gratitude. As more individuals around me were receiving the Holy Spirit, I held my head back and up to the heavens with complete submission because I knew that I was seeking something specifically from God: an instruction.

The congregation settled following the instructions from Bishop Rogers and went into a chorus of buzzing murmurs—personal prayers—seeking the Lord for guidance, healing, and breakthrough. He continued with the formalities, then took a deep dive into his sermon of complete transformation. The atmosphere was pregnant with possibilities and expectations. Mine had been undergoing metamorphosis for the past eighteen months—a process of silent toiling—that had gotten all my ducks in a row but one. Should I go back to school to obtain my master's?

As I stood with complete reverence, pleading to God for an answer, various attendees were receiving their answers. *Lord, I will not stop pleading until you bless me. Where is my answer? You disrupted my journey with your instruction eighteen months ago, which has been quite challenging. I need an answer, Lord!*

I was deeply committed—clinging onto my promise for dear life. I heard nothing, just a loud buzzing chorus of noise as though I was submerged underwater. Then it happened...

Bishop was pointed in my direction and said, 'Someone in the audience, over in that section. **God said to go to university. It will be OK**. Who am I speaking to?'

*That's me! That's the answer that I have been waiting on!*

So, I raised my hand. Then Bishop Rogers repeated his statement. 'God said to go to university; it will be OK.'

The congregation erupted into a chorus emanating sweet and joyous harmonies that filled the building.

I was in a trance. No one knew of my internal battle. I had secured a place on the MSc Business with Consulting course at Warwick University one year and seven months ago, and everything that could have gone wrong went wrong after receiving my confirmation letter.

I cried out joyfully because this was the answer I had been seeking, and here it was being delivered.

*This is for me. Thank you, Lord!*

I believed it, and I claimed that it would be OK. It had to be God. I have worked diligently to secure a position in an Ivy League business school, and all I needed was confirmation from God that I was on the right track.

*'Lord, thank you! You came at the last minute, of the last hour, through the last speaker delivering the last sermon. You are always on time!* I reflected as I poured my gratitude on my knees at my chair during the remainder of convention.

Three weeks later, my belongings were packed and squashed into luggage of all sizes, with complete conviction, holding onto nothing but the audacity of faith. Faith that everything will work together for my good, and the hope that all my dreams will come to fruition. My decision was solidified by the confirmation delivered by Bishop Rogers.

Cruising along the A4114 motorway, the GPS said, 'Take a left on Short Street.' From here, it took a little under twenty minutes to arrive at my destination—Little Heath—a leafy suburb of Coventry. This accommodation is in a residential house that belongs to my aunt's friend. Upon discovering the decline of my loan application earlier that day, I made a few phone calls en route. I learnt that my aunt's friend Suzette had a property she rented to Coventry University students. As luck may have it, a student vacated one of the rooms one month ago.

With only £3,000.00 in my account, I needed a job as soon as possible to clear the remainder of my tuition fee— £9,686.21 and pay my rent, food, and other amenities. So, as I dragged my belongings up the stairs to the vacant room, I was humbled because what looked like a closed door turned out to be an open window. As I placed my laptop on the antique desk adjacent to the bed, I was exhausted and overwhelmed.

This accommodation may be new to me, but these people are not. They are practically family, and I stayed at Suzette's daughter's home in London for almost two years while my mother was in prison. I can thrive here. Now, all I need is a job, so tomorrow, I will pass out the few CVs I brought with me, but only after checking the recruitment agencies I initially applied to. *Hopefully, I will get something sooner rather than later.* I reflected as I tried to get used to the spring-riddled mattress.

The next day, the phone alarm woke me up at 05:30 a.m. The springy mattress made it difficult to sleep all night. The twists and turns resulted in a strain on the right of my neck. To remedy this, I stood under warm running water for five minutes.

## 10:20 a.m. Friday Morning

After speaking with the final recruitment agency, the statement 'Unfortunately, we do not have vacancies at this time, but we can hold onto your CV, and we will contact you if the position is made available' became a recurring statement like a horrible theme song now being repeated by Mr Dennis, a recruitment consultant that I had been speaking with for the last eighteen minutes.

Like a broken record, all the recruitment agencies I rang today had no roles I could apply for. *I need a job! You know what—I am going to see if there are any vacancies on campus. At least I could work between classes or after to make ends meet.*

After pounding the pavement for what seemed like hours, I arrived at a standstill. Although I rang the agency that provides the supermarket with staff this morning, with a crispy CV and a huge smile, I confidently strut into Rootes Groceries.

'Good afternoon! I would like to speak to the manager, please.'

'Hello, I will check for you. Unfortunately, a manager is not available, but there is a supervisor. Would you like to speak with her?'

'Yes, please.'

'Hiya, my name is Becky. I am the supervisor on duty. Can I help?'

'Yes, you can. My name is Samantha, and I will be starting my induction on campus next week, but I am desperately in need of a job. I was wondering if you have any vacancies. I have a little over four years of retail experience. Although it may not be specifically obtained within a supermarket environment, they are transferable skills that I believe will help me be an asset within the team and the store. I have experience in merchandising and working on the till. I am flexible and willing to do whatever to be a great teammate.'

'We usually obtain new recruits from The Cove Agency. Give them a call and sign up to them so that they can keep you on file for when we need staff. I believe that both positions were filled last week. So, there aren't any vacancies currently available', said Becky.

'Please, I'm desperate! I arrived here from London late last night. I will work any shift. I am hardworking and a great team player.'

'Do you have a CV with you?'

Handing Becky my CV, I had a good feeling. This is my last chance, and as this store is positioned in the centre of campus, its convenience would be the best option.

'I will keep an eye out for you and will get in touch if anything comes up.'

'Thank you so much, Becky; that is greatly appreciated.'

*Well, I have given my CV to all the venues on campus. Lord, you said everything will be OK, so have your way,* I concluded while walking towards the bus terminus.

## 09:00 a.m. Saturday Morning

A sharp pain shot up the back of my neck, knocking me out of slumber just as my alarm was sounding. As I reached under my pillow, the weight of exhaustion overpowered me, and the dizziness from rising quickly caused me to slowly return to bed until the room stopped spinning. Pain pulsated along the back of my leg as a reminder of searching for a job the day before.

I moaned with disbelief. Two months ago, I had a job that I liked somewhat that paid my bills, and now I was in a foreign environment, jobless and discouraged.

*Lord, I don't know how you're going to do this, but you said, "...it will be OK...".*

Closing my eyes, I was awoken twenty minutes later by my phone vibrating.

'Hello!'

'Hi, can I speak to Samantha?'

'Yes, this is she. How may I help you?

'Hi, Samantha, this is Rebecca Staine (Becky) from yesterday at Rootes Groceries. Are you still looking for a part-time role?'

'Hi, Becky! Yes, I am!'

'We currently have a six-hour shift. I enjoyed talking with you yesterday; you were energetic and optimistic, so when this availability came up, I wanted to give you first refusal. I know that it's not much. It is the graveyard shift on Friday evenings from 18:00 p.m. – 00:00 a.m. I know it's only one shift, but this is a start for you to secure more shifts. What do you say, do you want it?'

'Yes, I'll take it for now, but hopefully, I could get more. I need between fifteen to thirty-four hours.'

'Well, I will keep an eye out for you.'

'Thank you, Becky. So, I'll be starting next Friday?

'Yes, correct. You can come in earlier to get your shirts. Just make sure that you are wearing black work trousers and a comfortable black pump. Oh, one more thing, you need to get to The Cove Agency to give them a copy of your passport, P45 and last P60.'

'OK, I will. Thank you very much, Becky. I greatly appreciate it.'

Be relentless. Let the promise of God guide and direct your decisions. Remember, all things work together for those who love the Lord, good and bad. At times, you may have your heart set on an outcome, and in the blink of an eye, that entire plan explodes in your face. Do not quit. Keep going. Trust and believe it will make sense in the end.

**Watch and pray.**

Isaiah reminds us that the Lord is with us, and He will give us what we need at the right time. So, keep your blinkers on. Do not let the fear of others prevent you from chasing your dreams and purpose. Pray about it, but put in the work also because "Faith without works is dead."

---

*"Forget the former things; do not dwell on the past."*
*Isaiah 43:18*

---

# PERSPECTIVE

'Hi, Becky! How are you doing? Long time, where have you been?'

'Hi, Sam! I was on holiday. I went to Marbella with my partner. It was our anniversary.'

'Oh, OK. Happy anniversary! Is Marbella in Spain, and how many years were you celebrating?'

'Yes, it is. It's our nine-year anniversary. We wanted to relax and chill by the pool.'

'That is brilliant! So, what did you get on your ninth wedding anniversary?'

'No. Sorry, Sam, I think you're confused. I'm not married—at least not yet. We have been together for nine years. I'm still waiting for him to propose...time is passing', said Becky with a melancholic expression on her face.

'Sorry, Becky! I didn't mean to pry. I simply assumed that as you said anniversary, you were talking about your wedding, albeit I haven't seen a ring on your finger.'

'Don't worry about it, Sam. I guess we were simply talking past each other. Anyway, once I get that ring, I will wear it always.'

'Fingers crossed; you will get it soon.'

'Thanks, Sam.'

'So, Becky, what area do you want me to focus on?'

'Start with the school apparel. Replenish the missing sizes, mugs and any other ornaments that need to be replaced. Once you have completed that, come back to me, and I will determine what you should do next.'

'Can I have the key for the storage room, please?'

'Here you go.'

'Thanks.'

*This must be the store; it's the only one over here.* I concluded while I forced the key into the lock. It opened after a bit of resistance.

Walking through the door, the sight of packs of hoodies dispersed across the room looked like a volcano that recently erupted, spewing molten lava everywhere. As I rummaged through the piles of what appeared to be a small mountain of clothes, I noticed the sizes were all mixed up and unorganised.

*I can't successfully replenish the stock on the shop floor from this mess.* I considered it as I decided to arrange the stockroom. While working my way through the chaos, I threw all the stock on the floor.

*By starting with a blank slate, I will be able to work my way through this mess.* I concluded before throwing all the products to the ground. On the floor, I started to gather small stacks of blouses, hoodies, and more by their sizes, and while doing so, it took me back to the catalyst that initiated this journey.

### *Bet on Me*
***

'Sam, will you be staying late tonight?' asked Adam Smith, my interim manager, who had been hiking across Europe for twelve months and decided to work for my company for six months while he explored the United Kingdom with his partner.

'Yes, I am. I have two days left to get all this out to our clients and to update their accounts before Friday so that the accountants can commence month-end', I said poignantly as I stretched out over piles of pages on my knees on the floor.

'Adam, have you got a moment before you head out? I would like to speak with you.'

'Yeah, I have a few minutes.'

'Remember a few weeks ago when I pitched the redesigned billing process to you.'

'Yes, I remember.'

'I have been so inspired by it that I would like to do something like this for the rest of my life.'

'What do you mean? Improving billing processes?'

'No, improve business processes and systems.'

'Oh, that sounds good. Just make sure that you include the catalyst that inspired you to want to progress your career.'

'Yes, I will. Thanks.'


Arriving early Thursday morning, the office was graveyard silent. During this time, I had the chance to reflect on my plans for my life while sorting the unorganised documents before sending the rest to the remaining clients. Forty-five minutes later, Pat McDougall exited out of the lift and headed to his desk.

*This is my chance,* I thought as I jumped to my feet and headed in his direction while there were three of us in the office.

'Good morning, Pat! You are in earlier today.'

'Can I ask you a massive favour, please?' I pleaded. 'Can you give me a reference? I have decided to return to university to complete my master's to redirect my career. After the improvements that I have made to our billing system, I am confident that this is the path that I want to take. I want to focus on the improvement of business performances.'

'Which universities have you applied for?'

'Manchester Metropolitan University and Warwick Business School.'

'Are you sure that you will get in?'

'Yes, most definitely. I have the grades and the experience, and I have spent some time working on my personal statement, which I am quite proud of.'

'OK, I will ask Gary to give you a reference.'

'You will!? Why him?'

'He is an alumnus from Warwick Business School.'

'Really? Wow. Thank you very much, Pat!' I exclaimed, astounded.

As I walked back to my desk, I was mesmerised with astonishment…

## Four Weeks Earlier

*Phone rings.*

'Good morning, you're through to Sam White. How may I help you?

'Hi Samantha, this is Johanna Myer, the internal training officer. I noticed that you had inputted an interest in receiving advanced Excel training. Are you still interested in it?'

'Hi Johanna, yes, very much!'

'Well, brilliant! We have an all-day training tomorrow, and there is one spot left. Do you want it?'

'I would love to, but I need to ask permission from my manager first. Could you please hold for me for ten minutes? I need to obtain permission first.'

'OK, please do respond as soon as possible because these spots are in high demand.'

'I will; give me five minutes', I said anxiously as I ended the phone call.

Looking around, Gary strolled past me. I hurried out of my chair to ask him permission to partake in the training.

I knocked on his office door and saw Gary mulling over some sheets.

'Come in', announced Gary as he slowly withdrew his attention away from the work to connect with me.

'Hi, Gary. I just got off the phone with a Johanna Myer who is currently holding a place for me on the Excel training course scheduled for tomorrow. I need your permission to sign up for the course. I have completed the majority of my tasks, and I will work overtime tonight to make sure that everything is completed. I need your permission now. I can't wait.'

Gary was the finance director of my department. He was my manager's boss. So, he was the best person to ask for permission.

'Wait a minute, Sam. Let's go back to the beginning. Have you spoken to Pat about this?'

'He is in an all-day meeting, and I have not seen him since he left this morning to go to the other office by Tottenham Station. I need this training, Gary. I will make sure that all my work for tomorrow is completed tonight.'

'Even if I give you permission, you must let Pat know as soon as possible.'

'Yes, I will. So, is it a yes?'

'It is a yes, assuming that you let Pat know.'

'Thanks, Gary! I will.' I reassured him as I exited his office and headed for my desk.

Grabbing the phone, I quickly identified Ms Myer's phone number and called her.

'Hi, Ms Myer. I got approved! I squealed.

'OK, I have put your name down. I will send you the course details in an email once I get off the phone. See you tomorrow.'

'Thank you so much, Ms Myer! See you tomorrow.'

Floating with excitement, I was doggedly focused with the aim of completing my month-end duties.

*I am shattered*! I thought, having generated invoices and statements non-stop for three hours. I decided to take my lunch as I was the last person in eyeshot who had not had my lunch, and it was two minutes to 16:00 p.m. So, I headed to the kitchen to heat up my lunch.

Fifteen minutes later, I returned to my desk and logged on to view *The Wendy Williams Show* online, my daily source of laughter and relaxation. As I slowly unwound with the therapy of laughter, Gary rushed past me. Not overthinking it, I continued to watch my program and consume my lunch.

A few minutes later, Gary and Pat emerged from the kitchen and walked towards Gary's office. Too engrossed in my program to care as, in my mind, I wasn't mentally there—I was mentally and legally on my lunch—albeit an overdue one at that. So, as Pat stormed towards me, I did not give it much thought and continued enjoying my lunch.

As I turned to my right, Pat shouted at me—about what I did not know.

'How many times have I told you not to sign up for courses!?' Pat screamed at me.

He continued, nose flaring and arms frantically animated. Like something out of a movie, I had a delayed response. Due to the headphones over my ears, I received bits of what he was annoyed about. I wasn't sure because I was on my lunch, and that was all that mattered to me at that moment.

On my second glance, his cheeks were fuchsia pink as though he was about to explode, so I grabbed my headphones out of my ear to give him my full attention.

'Pat, what is the matter?'

'Why did you sign up for the course?' he shouted.

'Because I want to improve my skillset so that I can progress in my career', I said, matter-of-factly.

'I told you to stop doing that!' he squealed.

'You were in a meeting all day, and I could not miss this opportunity. I have been waiting for this course to be reinstated for three months. And when the HR lady rang me, I could not forego the opportunity.'

'Why didn't you ask me?' he barked.

'I am on my lunch. When I finish, I was going to tell you', I said calmly as everyone in the office glared at us in awe.

Pat stared at me with disgust. With no response, he stormed off towards the lift as I continued to eat my lunch—after all, I was still on lunch and determined to enjoy it.

Fifteen minutes later, he walked past me with a cigarette in his mouth and a packet in his left hand and headed towards the back of the office where the smoking area was.

*Small victory*, I thought as I giggled to myself.

## Four Weeks Later

*I am so happy that I held my composure; had I not, I would not be here now.*

Walking back to my desk, I was hopeful but a little perturbed. Pat asking me if I would get into the universities I had applied to, annoyed me.

'Who does he think he is asking me that question?' I murmured.

Not being able to develop my skillset was one of the reasons why I wanted to move on. I felt my talents were not effectively utilised, and I wanted more. I wanted a career that challenged me, and I was elated to jump out of bed for every morning. Recently, I have been going through the motions, doing the same mundane activities that month-end required, and I was bored.

However, it was in my dream that I received the download that I should return to university. The crazy thing is I had no idea what I would study or where I would go. I simply had the dream at the start of January. To obtain more details from this instruction, I fasted for the remainder of the twenty-one days: Daniel's Fast. This fast is usually good for me because I tend to receive some transformative revelations for the upcoming year during this period.

Although I had received the instruction to return to university, I was somewhat dubious. My immigration status was still uncertain. This year, my three-year extension would end, totalling six years, which qualified me to apply for Indefinite Leave to Remain, but you never knew because the UK government likes to alter the rules every March.

*God has never failed me yet, so I will walk by faith.*

Boom, boom, boom! Sounds at the door.

'Samantha! Sam? Are you OK in there?' shouted Becky as she scampered into the storeroom.

Jolting back to the present, I saw Becky bent over me with a contorted face.

'Sam? Are you OK? Did you fall? What are you doing on the floor? I have been knocking on the door for over five minutes.'

'Hey, Becky! I must have dozed off. I'm on the floor because I wanted to sit down here while I arrange all the stock by style and size, and it was easier to do it on the floor. Sitting down here took me back to a job that required me to sit on the floor, which led to my return to uni.'

'Take a fifteen-minute break, then come back and finish the task. I'll close this door to prevent anyone from entering', said Becky.

'Thanks, Becky!'

I rose to my feet to have my break.

Do not share your dreams and aspirations with people you would not take advice from. Stay true to yourself and your intent and purpose. Hold them close to your chest until you have achieved them. People will use their insecurity and jealousy to re-route you down a path that kills your dreams.

***If you dream it, you can be it!***

Stay focused like a horse on a racecourse running his race. Keep your blinders on.

How? Time management—time is the only resource you can never recover. Do not waste it. Be accountable. Have monthly and quarterly reviews—with yourself, your friends, parents, teachers, relatives, mentors, or coaches. Have an accountability partner.

"For God hath not given us the spirit of fear but of
power, and of love, and of a sound mind."
2 Timothy 1:7

# SECOND CHANCE

'Hey, Sam, wait a minute; let me close the stockroom door.'

'OK?'

'What did you mean when you said, "...the last job required you to sit on the floor, which led you to return to uni?"'

'Well...I worked in the media industry in a popular media firm. I liked working there, but my attempts to progress were being stifled by a manager who didn't want me to acquire additional skills that would warrant me demanding more pay. After eighteen months of working there, I used my initiative to redesign one of their system processes that was causing a massive bottleneck the last week of the month. It was successful and the catalyst that ignited my desire for more in my life.'

## *Catalyst*
***

'Sam!' squealed Kenny as she entered the kitchen. Kennysia is my Filipino-Spanish work colleague who started working at this establishment four months ago. She has been a ray of sunshine with a matching personality and just what I needed in this dreary time.

'Hey, hun. What's up?'

'Have you seen the email?'

'What email?'

'Gary sent out a congratulatory email highlighting to the team the system improvement you made to the billing process. Congratulations, Mama! Well done. You deserve it', she said as we hugged and jumped around in the tiny staff kitchen.

'Amazing! I can't believe he announced it', I screamed. I was beaming.

This atmosphere starkly contrasted with where I was almost seven months ago.

### Seven Months Earlier

'Good morning, ladies!' said Pat.

'Good morning, Pat', we chorused.

'I called this impromptu meeting to inform you that Aaron has terminated his contract.'

'REALLY! Why?' shouted Arin in shock. 'Why? What happened?'

We were all staring at Pat in complete confusion, except me.

'His partner had a horrible experience with her last pregnancy, and due to that, she has renegotiated with her company to be relocated back to Australia so that she can be close to her family. Aaron wanted to be by his family's side, which is the honourable thing to do—hence his resignation.'

'Oh, that makes sense. Well, let him know we will miss him!' said Arin, and all my other colleagues agreed, except me.

'Who will be our manager now that Aaron is gone?' I asked Pat.

'Well, it is going to have to be me while we find Aaron's replacement', confirmed Pat reluctantly.

*Thank you, Lord!* I thought and gave a massive sigh as we strolled back to our desks.

## Six Months Earlier

'Good morning, Sam. How are your abs coming along? I would like to see them soon.' Aaron's message popped up in my inbox.

*Not today, devil,* I thought, seeing one of his umpteen messages. I rolled my eyes and decided not to respond to it.

*The audacity of this man. His partner just had a baby a few weeks ago. This is his first day back off paternity leave. What the hell is wrong with him?*

I continued to do my work, converse with other colleagues, and avoid him.

Aaron Justen was my manager. A biracial New Zealander—Māori and White—with a South Italian mahogany skin tone, he was an ex-rugby player with deceivingly kind eyes and still had a thick head of curly hair, though it was 95 per cent grey.

'Is there anything wrong with the internet? I think I may be having connection issues', Aaron asked another colleague.

Upon hearing his question, I quietly excused myself from my desk to make a cup of coffee in the kitchen to avoid the stares he was darting in my direction.

'Lord, I have been praying to you for some time now. I don't know how much of this I can take. I need your help with this situation', I whispered just before exiting the kitchen and returning to my desk. Sitting in my chair, I avoided his eye contact as he undressed me with his eyes.

'So, are you going to respond to my message?' popped up on my screen from Aaron. I deleted it and continued with my work.

On several occasions, I asked Aaron for training—advanced Excel and some accounting skills—and he was unwilling to do this without me agreeing to see him outside of work. This was not communicated to me explicitly, as he knew that doing so would warrant his being fired. So, I decided to play chess while he was playing checkers. I smiled and had small conversations to keep him disarmed. I did not file any complaints against him; I simply ignored him whenever he tested me with inappropriate advances, comments, and gestures. He even tried to persuade me with his property portfolio and his net worth.

Having been raised around older people, I pitied him because he didn't know I realised his partner wore the trousers in their relationship. I never reported him because I realised that he was a broken man. Through continuous communication, I knew he felt trapped by his children's mother, a smart, savvy businesswoman who did not want anything from him but his genes. She was self-sufficient, had a full life, and only decided to contact him when approaching her forties and wanted to have children. He confirmed that he was single then, and she wooed him and locked him into a relationship with her womanly charms.

However, it did not make him any wiser. I pretended I didn't recognise his inappropriate advances. So, feeling powerless, he wanted to impose his manhood over a young and naïve female. But being forty-eight years old to my twenty-seven years, he was ignorant of my worldly knowledge.

After six months of ignoring his subtle inappropriate advances, comments, and gestures *through* prayer and fasting, he was moved out of my path to Australia.

'Thank you, Lord. You are always on time', I murmured as I sat at my desk.

Hopefully, I will have a better manager that will inspire me to dig deep to reach my full potential.

## Two Weeks Later

'Good morning, all!'

'You are in a good mood. What's up?' asked Sheila, a credit controller who was a part of another team within the finance department.

'I'm simply in a good mood. The weather is good, and right now, I am happy with that', I replied.

*I'm just happy that I don't have to deal with Aaron anymore. Good riddance.*

Logging back onto my desktop, the email below popped up.

## 11:39 a.m.

'Hi, Sam,

I hope that you are doing well. I arrived safely if you were wondering. I am now officially a stay-at-home dad. When I initially took the girls to the new parents' group playdates, the mothers all thought that my partner was a man...lol. Can you believe it?

So, how's the workout regimen coming along? I am planning to return to the UK in three months. It would be nice to see you. We can go for a drink—near my Knightsbridge property. Would you be up for that?

I'm looking forward to seeing you again.

Aaron'

'Arrgghh', I moaned frustratedly.

'That's loud, Sam. What's up?' enquired Kennysia.

'I cannot deal with this. This man has been pressuring me for almost twelve months. Even being on the other side of the world doesn't stop him. I am not responding; I don't care. I have had enough of it', I responded frustratedly.

'Eventually, Aaron took the hint I wasn't interested. He made my working life a living hell. Aaron caused a lot of chaos within the team—all females. Being the only male on the team, he pitted us against each other and caused the six of us to split into two groups. On several occasions, he would take the team with Arin on lunch meetings, which caused resentment. It was so bad that even Pat noticed the tension between us.

'I know that he did that because he wanted to bed me. He acted like I rejected him, as though he was eligible for a relationship with me. He was in a twelve-year relationship with the mother of his children, although he didn't marry her.'

*There is no way I could ever trust him.*

'So, I decided to not respond; hopefully, he would get the picture.

'Three weeks after his departure, I was introduced to an interim manager, an Australian, who was travelling across the UK. He would be working with us for one to two months until a permanent manager was found. Through his encouragement, I designed a new billing procedure for my organisation. With his encouragement, I pitched it to senior management—Pat—who agreed to it if it didn't cost any extra money.

'A week later, it was done. I pitched it to my manager, who was impressed and persuaded me to present it to Pat, who was happy with it. The next day, I relayed my idea to one of the IT technicians who realised my concepts. And yes, it was announced to the department by the finance director, Gary. This was when Kenny rushed into the staff kitchen to reveal the news.

'This was my catalyst, something that made me excited to go to work. My second chance to unveil my true potential and purpose. So, with the wind under my sail, I was motivated to apply to university to commence my studies. After one week of research and prayer, I settled on Warwick and Manchester universities as their master's programmes complemented the skillsets I need to become the consultant I hope to be.

'After approaching Pat and asking him to write a reference for me, he confirmed that he would ask his manager, Gary, the finance director. I was totally optimistic that this was the start of my journey. After I submitted my application, as promised, Gary submitted his reference. Although I was in the dark about what was written, I was confident it was good because I have gone above and beyond in this role and have recently improved the billing process. Even though my undergraduate studies were traumatic, I am still hopeful and hope to utilise all the lessons I learned then and now. With all those things considered, I hoped this was my second chance.'

'Wow! Sam, that is a lot. Why didn't you tell someone you were being sexually harassed?' said Becky.

'I didn't care too much because he wasn't explicit with it. So, I pretended to be naïve and ignored his advances.'

'Well, I'm floored. You have been through so much. Go and enjoy your break', she said.

'Thanks a lot, Becky. I'm going to have a cup of tea and a sausage roll.'

Every new day is an opportunity to make a difference and impact someone's life. You do so by renewing your mind, and the renewal of your mind is made possible through forgiveness. Forgiveness is the means that allows you to start from scratch with a clean slate. A clean slate lets you step back from a situation and see it with fresh eyes and a new perspective.

**_Forgive, but do not forget._**

No man is perfect. Do not forget past transgressions because they help you navigate similar problems. Similarly, forgiveness is crucial in tackling situations because Matthew reminds you that it is good to forgive those who have wronged you because He will forgive you of your sins consequently.

---

*"For if you forgive other people when they sin against you, your heavenly Father will also forgive you." Matthew 6:14*

---

# REVELATION

# NEW PASTURES

'Hey, Sam! What were you working on?' questioned Neil, a night supervisor.

'I was replenishing the University accessories. For me to effectively do this, I decided to rearrange the stockroom. It was a mess in there.'

'Have you finished that task?' he asked.

'Yeah, I only just finished, but everything is nice and tidy and clean, just how I like it. Where is Becky? Is it that time already?' I asked.

'Yep. She finished for the day.'

'Cool, OK. I mean, she could have said goodbye. I was probably stuck in the stockroom. I'll see her next time.'

'Are you working until midnight?' said Neil.

'Yep, same as usual. I'm here until the store closes. What would you like me to focus on next?'

'The Oriental aisles look a bit sparse. Follow me. Let's see what's in the storeroom.'

'OK, I'm right behind you', I confirmed while I strolled behind him.

Neil was the youngest supervisor on the team, an Indian whose facial features reminded me of my old manager at the media company, who joined nine months before I was booted out.

### Frozen
***

Four months later, Adam Smith, my interim manager, moved to Europe to continue his trek across that continent. Additionally, my close friend Kennysia left as she was unsatisfied with her role.

*I miss my girl, Kenny,* I reflected as I strolled past the vacant chair where she used to be positioned on my way to the kitchen to make my first cup of coffee for the day.

Returning to my desk, Pat announced that management had settled on a new manager to be accountable for my department.

'Good morning, ladies! I bring good news.'

'What's the good news, Pat?' shouted Arin.

'I brought you new eye candy to whet your appetite! He is young, smart, and handsome. You will be happy with our choice,' said Pat.

'Where is he then?' asked Sheila.

'He should be here in twenty minutes,' said Pat. 'So, go back to your desk and get some work done. When he arrives, I will take you to one of the meeting rooms so that you can introduce yourselves to him.'

Returning to our desks, we did little work. We spent the next twenty minutes discussing and devising all the possible scenarios of what the new manager could look like.

Pat entering the office caused us to scamper back to our desks and pretend to be busy.

'I know that you were not working. Well, the wait has now come to an end. The manager's name is Charles— Charles Jefferson. He is currently making his way up the elevator', he announced, giggling with a twinkle in his eyes.

*As long as he is good at his job, I am not fussed with his physical appearance.*

I settled while I typed a response to one of our internal account managers.

Re-reading the email, I felt happy with its content, so I clicked the SEND button to submit it. Feeling satisfied with my decision, I quickly glanced around the office from right to left and back. Returning left, I saw a gentleman emerge from the lift.

*Tall, debonair, athletic, and well-dressed. He must be Mr Jefferson.* Clothed in a light blue, perfectly ironed shirt and navy blue trousers, he strutted along the pathway, and while walking, our eyes locked.

*Oh no! Whatever you do, avoid eye contact. You do not want any attraction to arise between you and your manager. You do not want to relive that last painful experience that occurred between you and Aaron.* I quickly looked away. Then, as he looked away, I quickly took another glance at him.

'Freckles, dimples, and a brilliant smile...oh, Lord!' I murmured. That combination is my kryptonite.

Simultaneously, all the ladies on our team turned their heads in his direction and slurped him up like dehydrated people on an extremely humid day.

*I must avoid him at all costs because I'm attending university this autumn to read for my master's. I don't have time for any distraction—no matter how good he looks or how perfect he may be for me.*

'OK, ladies! Let's congregate in meeting room two in five minutes so that you can introduce yourselves individually to your new manager', Pat instructed.

After Pat made the announcement, we all rushed to the toilet. In this moment of frenzy, we spruced ourselves up while showing off among each other.

'Who has face powder? Perfume, can I borrow some? OMG!! Did you see him? He is stunning!' We all erupted in chorus in agreeance. The toilet was pandemonium.

Hair accessories, makeup, and perfume filled the atmosphere.

'It's time to go!' shouted Sara.

Woooww!! Sounds of chitter-chatter filled the air as we all flowed out of the toilet towards meeting room two.

*Avoid eye contact, avoid eye contact*! I repeated to myself as anxiety gripped my stomach while heading towards the room.

Entering meeting room two, most ladies positioned themselves directly in front of Charles. Arin pulled up a chair and sat a few inches from where he was standing. She even pulled up her dress to cross her legs, revealing bare skin. Simultaneously, Sara and I looked at each other in disbelief.

'What is she doing? She is not that desperate!' whispered Sara in my ear.

I responded with an 'I don't know' and a shrug. I could not conjure up any more information; I was too worried about my emotions, which were all over the place. Sara and I stood the furthest away from him—at the back of the room, away from his peripheral view.

*He ticks all the boxes on my list of what I prefer aesthetically in a partner. I do not mix business and pleasure, so stay away from him. And Sam, do not look him in his eyes*! I said to myself while he introduced himself to us as a group.

The room erupted in laughter, and to appear present, I smiled gingerly to remain polite.

Sporting black spandex leggings and a three-toned striped flowy top with a pair of black-heeled ankle boots pulled together with deep red lipstick, I was looking and feeling trendy. The red lipstick was in stark contrast with my white teeth. Looking around the room, Charles's smiling face collided with mine, and our eyes met. The air left the room. A wave of electric energy transferred between us, though we were on opposite sides of the room, and immediately, I knew I was in trouble.

Sara glanced at him and then at me. She felt it. Immediately, I broke our connection by looking at Sara.

*Oh shoot, I'm in trouble! AVOID HIM! AVOID HIM, SAM! DO EVERYTHING TO AVOID HIM!* I screamed in my head. I was anxious, and nothing else that he said registered with me. The room was caving in, and all I wanted to do was leave. So, the moment we were dismissed, I headed straight for the door, avoiding eye contact with Mr Jefferson.

Returning to our desk, the ladies could not help but fuss over him. Sara was a little quiet, but she joined in on the conversations. On the other hand, I stayed busy to avoid conversations about him.

We were all single, and all of us (except me) were vying for his attention, though we didn't know if he was single.

Over the course of the day, he had one-to-one introductory talks with us, except for me. I kept busy so that I would appear unavailable for his address.

After speaking with everyone, he strolled over to my desk, which was the furthest from his in the corner, past all the other ladies' desks. While walking towards me, everyone's heads popped up like meerkats, recognising danger.

'Hiya, I need to speak with you. Are you free now, or should we talk later?' asked Charles.

'I'm in the middle of an email. I'll come and find you once I finish.'

Unfortunately, he had back-to-back meetings that prevented him from having our one-on-one talk that day.

Five o'clock p.m. crept up on us, and he was nowhere to be found, so I went home.

The following day made no difference. Everyone was vying for his attention, and as I wanted to avoid his presence, his high demand came as a blessing. I kept my head down whenever he wandered over to our cubicle to say hello and check on us.

After lunch, he strutted over to me. 'Sammy, Sammie, Sam! How are you? Do you need any help?'

'No, I am fine', I replied indifferently.

'Are you sure?' replied Charles in a jovial manner.

The table was silent. Everyone was listening to our conversation.

Not one to draw attention to myself, I replied frostily, 'I am fine. I'm simply getting on with my work.' I needed him to walk away from my desk because I did not want to compete with anyone, and besides, I don't mix business with pleasure.

He looked me in the eye. I made a head gesture for him to go and cracked a small smile. I believe he understood, so he returned to his desk.

## Friday Morning

I arrived early Friday morning like I usually do. I like to get to work at 08:00 a.m. so I can get most of my work done by 16:00 p.m. when we go for happy hour as a team at the pub around the corner from the office.

Donning a flowy floral dress paired with sheer leggings and black-studded ankle boots, I was looking and feeling pretty. My hair was freshly done in a curly updo, too.

Exiting from the lift, the office was empty.

*Yay, just how I like it*! I thought. I was smiling because I was the first employee in the office, so I did a little jig approaching my desk. *Right! Let me get on with my day. I must get on with my tasks. I want to enjoy happy hour.*

Quickly popping into the kitchen, I made a cup of coffee before the other employees arrived.

Eight minutes later, Charles swaggered from the lift. Walking to his desk, we exchanged formalities, and then I went straight back to work. However, logging onto one of the accounting software I usually use was a struggle, so I asked Charles for guidance.

'Hi Charles, can I ask you for some advice?'

'Yes, Sam. What's up?'

'I have been trying to log onto Sage for almost fifteen minutes now with no luck. What do you think I should do?'

'You may need to contact IT, as I am still familiarising myself with the organisation's software, and as such, I don't want to give you incorrect information.'

'OK, I appreciate your honesty. They are not available until 09:00 a.m. I'm going to have to do something else until I can give them a call.'

'You OK with everything else?'

'I am, thanks', I said with a smile.

'You are friendlier today, why is that?' enquired Charles as he stood up.

With a nervous smile, I stepped back slightly and stared up at him awkwardly. Struggling to focus on the words coming out of his mouth, I felt the oxygen being sucked out of my body.

The sparks that flew between us for two days were magnetic, and the energy between us was pulling us together. As I retreated from his advances, I became stuck between Charles leaning into me and the column that stood beside his desk.

*What is he doing? I don't mix business with pleasure! BUSINESS WITH PLEASURE!*' I was screaming in my head, but the words could not leave my mouth.

Simultaneously, Charles started biting his lips and looking at me seductively. Frozen and shocked, I was trapped. As he continued to move towards me, my words failed me. Nothing.

With my eyes screaming at him, '*WHAT ARE YOU DOING?*', I kept shouting at him in my head, but the words were locked in the prison of my mind and body. My toes curled, my chest tightened, and my breathing slowed. I froze.

Lips quivering, eyes lusting, and as his eyes scanned mine, he came back to himself inches from my lips. He caught himself as he realised what he was about to do was unethical and illegal. I felt the electricity that rushed between us, but I did not act on it. He did. With no reciprocation, he broke eye contact and hastily walked away.

*Thank God no one is in the office to see what happened,* I thought as I exhaled. Shaken, I fixed my dress and then walked back to my desk. Sitting down, I quickly scanned the floor to locate Charles. To my shock, Steve was hunched over at his desk! Avoiding eye contact, he pretended to be busy.

*Wow! He saw everything that just happened. Steve just saw everything that took place, and he did not intervene. What a jerk!* I contemplated.

Shamed, I kept my head down and got on with work until 10:00 a.m. when breakfast arrived. Over the day, Charles avoided me. It was awkward, and we avoided each other in every situation. Happy hour was far from *happy*!

'Sam, Sam, SAM!' shouted Neil while waving a hand across my face.

'Are you OK! That was scary, man.'

'What was crazy?'

'Your eyes were open, but no one was home. I couldn't get a reaction from you. I have been calling you for almost five minutes.'

'I believe I was daydreaming. It's strange; I need to get some sleep because my present is being interrupted by my past.'

'What do you mean by that?' Neil asked.

'Don't worry about it, it's not important. Earlier, I had a look at the water; it needs replenishing. I'll work on that until my fifteen-minute break, which is coming up in thirty minutes.'

'Cool; I'll get the water cage', said Neil.

Three minutes later, Neil returned to the shop floor, hauling behind him a cage filled with 50 cl and 75 ml bottles of water in various brands.

'Thanks, Neil!'

'No worries, I'm just doing my job.'


Hold steadfast to your goals, but be flexible about how you get there. There is a popular phrase that says when you plan, God laughs. Life is a rollercoaster; remain optimistic and take every loss as a lesson learnt.

**Stay hungry and eager!**

Keep a childlike mindset. Remain hungry for knowledge and new opportunities. Philippians reminds us to not be anxious about anything. Stay hungry and treat every opportunity as your last—give it your best shot—and if you are unsure about your purpose, stay focused and remain excited; your purpose will reveal itself naturally.

---

*"Do not be anxious about anything, but in every situation, by prayer and petition, with thanksgiving, present your requests to God." Philippians 4:6*

---

# THE REVELATION

* * *

*I am starving! What time is it?* I thought.

Checking the clock at the centre of the store, I registered that it was 14:47 p.m. 'Wow! Where did the time go?!' I murmured.

I rapidly walked back to where I was working and took two steps back to assess my work. I quickly walked up and down the aisle to review the alignment of the soft drinks. I saw it was good, so I piled all the remaining stock onto the cage and pushed it back into the stockroom. After fighting with the cage, I returned to the aisle to collect the plastic bags and cardboard boxes to dispose of them in the recycle cages in the back of the store.

Struggling to balance with stacked boxes in my arms caused me to walk into a customer.

'Heeyyy!' screamed a soft voice flowing from behind the stacks of boxes as they exploded to the ground, scattering everywhere.'

'Oh, no! I didn't see you there. I am so sorry', I said frantically.

We stared at each other defencelessly, then erupted in laughter.

'Haha, that is hilarious! The way those boxes launched and scattered over the floor was awesome.'

'I am so sorry! I truly didn't see you.'

'It's OK. I know that I am small, and it is obvious that this was an accident. Don't worry about it.'

'Thank you! I'm so sorry about this again!' I said apologetically while manically dragging the plastic bags and cardboard boxes into a corner with my feet as I held on to the stack balanced in my hands.

Rushing out the back, I disposed of the rubbish and returned immediately to scoop up the remnants.

Strolling into the restroom, I stumbled upon Fatima as she was heading in the opposite direction.

'Hey, Sam! How are you?' she blurted out with a cheesy grin.

'Hey, Fatima! I am doing OK. A little tired, but I'm managing.'

'By the skin of your teeth, eh?'

'Something like that, I guess.'

'I need to use the Ladies.'

'OK, see you out there.'

'Yes, see you on the shop floor.'

Thirty minutes later, on my way back to the shop floor, I scanned the rota to see who the Sunday evening manager and supervisors were: Tracy and Fatima. Yes! I celebrated. This evening was going to be quite productive.

Stopping at the cashier, I asked Neil whether Tracy was in. He explained that he had not seen her and was unsure if she was in today.

'She is, or at least she will be. I checked the rota. She may be running late.'

'Yeah, maybe', Neil said nonchalantly.

'Where is Fatima?'

'She is in the stockroom.'

'OK, thank you.'


Entering the stockroom, I saw Fatima. She was on her phone, engrossed in a heated conversation. Glancing at my face, she paused.

Looking at her, I whispered, 'What do you want me to do next?'

'Stay in here and tidy it up. It's a mess', she said frankly before bolting out of the room to continue her conversation.

*Well, seeing as I'm going to be here, I might as well get my phone and listen to some music.*

Two minutes later, returning to the warehouse, I heard some shouting outside. Being inquisitive, I cracked the back door to see what was going on.

'I have spent too much time under...' The shouting stopped.

'Oops', I tiptoed back into the warehouse.

*It sounded like Fatima, but I'm not sure, so I will put my earbuds in and mind the business that pays me.* I settled before putting some music on.

*Most families are complicated. That's why you can't be jealous of what you believe another person has. Their family life could seem wonderful when you are outside looking in, but being in the middle of it could be your worst nightmare. It is better to struggle and be grateful for the family that you have. You were added to it for a reason.* I reflected.

'Better the evil, you know', I whispered.

*Well, let's do this!* I said emphatically to psych myself up, and then I skipped through to find a song that energised me.

### Melted
***

'Sam! Do you think Charles is handsome? Do you fancy him?' asked Sheila jovially.

'I don't see him like that.'

'If I was ten years younger, I'd be all over him.'

'Sheila, if you were ten years younger, what difference would it make? Do you know how old he is? What if he is in a relationship? What type of person piques his interest?'

'I probably wouldn't do a thing', she confessed.

Looking at her, I couldn't help but feel a little sorry for her. We were a team of females of all ethnicities, qualities, and styles. At least one of us could be his type—if he were looking. I will not wait around yearning for someone I don't even know if he is single.

The following week, Charles avoided me, and when we shared small spaces, especially for meetings, he overlooked me. I believe he was embarrassed and perhaps concerned that I would report him. I did not, though.

Later, I learned that he recently came out of a long-term relationship. He was thirty years old and of biracial heritage. His mother was White Irish, and his father was Black Caribbean. He was highly desired by all the women in the accounting department and other parts of the company.

The following two months were extremely awkward. We had a spiritual connection; I could not get Charles off my mind. He was my type in every way. The attraction between us was like a stench that would not evaporate. One night, I had an intense, inappropriate dream about us breaking office rules. I enjoyed it so much that it was hard to shake my attraction to him. Fighting to be released from the dream, tossing and turning, I rolled out of bed, hitting my head against my bedside table, jolting me out of sleep.

Discovering that I was accepted into both university programmes was the confirmation that I needed. This initiated the beginning of my detachment from the organisation and everyone in it. I was laser-focused. No one was going to derail my plans. I had no intention to deviate from my plans for any man, so I avoided him. I simply gave him the cold shoulder. His freckles, dimples, physique, and smile had me hypnotised, but I could not be distracted. I was determined to achieve my goal—the purpose I was born to accomplish.

Each day, work became more unbearable.

'Sara, do we have a team meeting this morning?' I asked politely.

'Yes, I believe so, but wait one minute, let me ask Charles. Actually, why don't you ask him directly?'

'I don't really want to', I reluctantly confessed.

'Sam, he is not going to bite! Just go. Go!' she said, pushing me in his direction.

'Excuse me, Charles, may I ask you a question?'

'Samantha, why so formal? I don't bite.'

'So, I was told', I said sheepishly, staring at him. His staring at me caused us to erupt in laughter.

'What do you want to know?' he asked awkwardly.

'Do we have a meeting today?'

'Yes, we do—a little under an hour', he replied.

'Thank you for confirming', I said hastily before rushing to my desk.

## 55 Minutes Later

'Thank you, ladies, for all being here on time. I've heard that you have some misconceptions about me. Now is the time to ask as many questions as you can cram in the next forty-five minutes.'

Charles opened up about most things, and towards the end of the session, we learnt where he obtained his undergraduate degree. Questions were never-ending. How many siblings do you have? Are you single? Are you looking to date?

That last question dragged me back into the room. I sat up taller and focused on hearing the answer with all the energy I could muster.

'So?' asked Arin.

'I recently broke up with my girlfriend of six years!'

I am open, and he is dating. I heard nothing else. Everything else that was mentioned got repelled from me. My ears were a positively charged vacuum, and his words were also positive. They simply bounced off.

*He is single and looking! I am not looking.*

*We are complete opposites. There is no way we could successfully unite, especially to bring children into this world!* I scream for joy in my head. My initial attraction towards him was a nuclear bomb that was detonated. A line was drawn not to be crossed.

The meeting ended, and walking out of the room, I could finally see a ray of sunlight making visible the path that I needed to focus on.

Two weeks had passed, and the tension between Charles and I had grown. The more I avoided him, the greater his chase—he was persistent.

As I walked towards the HR office, it was business as usual. I was summoned to the office. Having dealt with immigration woes for almost fifteen years, the procedure was embedded in my psyche. I could hear my solicitor saying, '...when you send your immigration documents to the Home Office for an extension, you remain in whatever circumstance you are in until the Home Office returns your documents with a decision...' I could practically outline the script structure the HR officer and I would exchange once we discussed this matter. Flashbacks of alternate scenarios filled me with triumph because I left the victor on previous occasions.

*I left a victor*! I reflected, donning optimism wrapped in a pretty bow of cheer as I entered the room as instructed by the receptionist.

'Good morning! My name is Samantha!'

'Morning, I know who you are', interjected the lady politely.

'So, you were invited to this meeting today because your Visitor Visa is about to expire.'

'Yes', I replied with a corresponding head shake.

'I have gone over your records, and they show that you are not a British citizen, and as such, you were booked in this meeting to discuss your immigration status and your future with us', stated the HR Officer.

'I understand, but I have been in this position twice before. On the last two occasions, I remained in the position that I was in until the Home Office returned with their decision.'

'This is a new situation for me. I have not dealt with your circumstance before', she replied.

'Yes, I understand, but I have. I sent off my documents three weeks ago. HMRC normally takes six months or more to decide.'

'OK. Well, I need some form of documentation that corroborates this and perhaps a letter from your solicitor. I will give you two weeks to do so, and, in the meantime, I will do some research, too.'

'OK, thank you for your time. I'll get on it now.'

'Right, I must go. I have another meeting in fifteen minutes', said the HR Officer.

The next few days were a nightmare. I was scrambling to get my documents together for my next HR meeting. Appointments with my solicitor were arranged and rearranged because of his workload, which I was able to secure one day before my HR follow-up meeting. I journeyed to Balham to retrieve the letter confirming that my application and documents had been sent to the Home Office to apply for my Indefinite Leave to Remain.

'Good morning, again.'

'Good morning.'

'Did you manage to obtain the information that I sent you in the email?'

'I did what I could. I have a letter from my solicitor and a confirmation letter from the Home Office dated the 18th of May 2016 that they have received my application. These are all I have.'

'I'm not sure if this is good enough. We need your passport. How long will the Home Office take?'

'They can take anywhere from six months to however long they want. It takes as long as it takes. Also, we are notified that we cannot contact them—only on the extenuating circumstance that one needs to leave the country on a time-sensitive basis, such as a funeral. Even that is subjective.'

'This is all new to me, Miss White. I must ask my manager for further information and will inform you of the outcome in an email.'

'Thank you again.'

'Hopefully, we will resolve this matter as soon as possible', concluded the HR officer.

'OK', I said while breathing deeply before exiting the room.

With thoughts dancing around my mind, the last thing I wanted to hear was any more of her excuses. *I know I am right—I have been here before, so why is she making this so difficult.*

The next day, the HR officer was in our building. She was not there to see me. As Charles was a new manager, there were several documentation matters and processes that he needed to go through with her.

Walking back from the kitchen with a cup of coffee, I encountered Charles.

'Good morning, Sam! How's it going?' said Charles.

'Good morning, Charles! I am OK, with all things considered.'

'What is the progress with your immigration issues?' he whispered.

'It's all up in the air, currently. The HR officer that you are in a meeting with now says she will email me with the outcome once she is instructed by her manager.'

'You mean Chloe Charter?' he asked.

'Is that her name?

'Yes. You have had two meetings with her and didn't know her name?'

'She never introduced herself, so I never bothered to pry. I figured once she emails me, her name will be on her signature.'

While in the middle of our conversation, I glanced in her direction, and she had an evident disposition. She looked uncomfortable—a cross between inquisitive and suspicious. *I don't know why; I'm not interested in Charles. Maybe she is.*

'Let me know the prognosis. I'm sure it will all work itself out in the end', said Charles as he strolled into the kitchen.

'Hopefully', I replied as I walked back to my desk with a slight smile at the thought of not having to deal with immigration anymore.

*It's been too long; I am tired. I have been living in this open prison for too long.* I thought as I strolled past the office where Chloe sat. Acknowledging her in the room, she returned a cold, distant stare. Not thinking anything of it, I continued with my day.

A few minutes later, Charles, walking past me, nodded with a smile, so I returned the same gesture and watched him as he entered the room. Glancing at Chloe, she produced an even colder stare to say, 'I'm watching you.'

*I guessed she wanted him for herself,* I decided before stepping back to reflect on my efforts.

'Well done, Sam. You've done an awesome job rearranging the stockroom. There's one more thing: give the floor a once-over', said Fatima as she entered the room.

'Okay, where is the broom? Ah, I found it.'

'Don't put too much effort into it; it's just a quick sweep.'

'Alright, Fatima, I will do; I'll do my best. What should I do next?'

Situations and people change, but you will remain constant. No man exists in a vacuum. You are either impacted by someone else's decisions, or your choices influence someone else's outcome.

**Vengeance is not yours.**

People are inherently selfish and are usually driven by gratification. When you are done wrong, get angry and cry if you need to, but do not try to take revenge. Romans reminds us that vengeance is the Lord's, so He will avenge your honour.

---

*"Beloved, never avenge yourselves, but leave room for the wrath of God; for it is written, "Vengeance is mine, I will repay, says the Lord.""" Romans 12:19*

---

# CATAPULTED

'Heeyy, Sam!'

'Heeyy, Tracy! I was wondering whether you were coming in or not.'

'I had to wait until my husband arrived home. He was running late, and you know how that goes. It caused a domino effect. After you finish stocking the small crisps, you are due for a fifteen-minute break. How much is left over?'

'Well, there are two small boxes of mixed crisps and half a box of large crisps that are overs.'

'Right, where are they? I'll take them back to the storeroom so that all you have to do is flatten the empty boxes and place them in the cages outside.'

'They are over there to the left beside the stationary shelves. Thanks, Tracy!' I replied with a complimentary smile.

After a few minutes of shoving the flattened boxes into the empty cages outside and rearranging empty trays for reuse by the suppliers, I was finished.

Looking around, it was a typical Sunday on campus, small groups of students scampering to their destinations—anywhere from dorm rooms, restaurants, cafés, and most importantly, the twenty-four-hour library where most students would be couped up completing various assignments.

Too exhausted to be resentful, I returned to the supermarket to have my fifteen-minute break. Feeling resentful was now a regular occurrence. Resentful about my current situation—constantly working to pay for my studies and only having the hours outside of work to study—early mornings until dusk sometimes—and managing to squeeze in approximately four hours of sleep.

Having to use almost all my waking hours to work to pay for my studies, I had fought hard only to get to university to work to pay for my studies. Nonetheless, giving up was not an option as this was not the only time I had fought against setbacks, especially when I was booted out of my role in the media company...

## Deception
***

'Sam, have you finished eating?' asked Sandra.

'Yeah, I'm just about to finish', I replied airily.

*I have been on my feet since 09:00 a.m., and it's now four minutes to 21:00 p.m. I should be heading home; I am sick and tired of working in a hair salon. I made an effort with a little extra foundation today. I even used extra hair gel and mascara. These are the only pleasures that I can enjoy at this moment.*

You have probably figured it out, but the tension within the office increased. The more I avoided Charles, the more he tried to get my attention. Some of my teammates wanted me to date him, but I vehemently declined.

Chloe was in our building more frequently, and observing the attraction that Charles had for me caused her to resent me further.

Two weeks after our meeting, she emailed me that I would have to resign temporarily until the Home Office returned my passport with the right to stay in the UK. Completely embarrassed, I waited until the office was practically empty before I boxed up my personal belongings and left the organisation.

Being entirely informed of my circumstances, Charles stayed behind and waited for me to gather my things together.

'Sam, I am truly heartbroken. If there was anything that I could do for you, I would.'

'Thanks, Charles, I know you would. Also, thank you for staying behind until I gathered my things.'

Exiting the lift on the first floor, he thanked me again, gave me a hug and some chocolates, and reassured me that I should contact him once I received my documents back from the Home Office.

'Thank you for everything, Charles. I will do.'

Walking into the lift heading to the ground floor, thoughts danced around my mind. How am I going to pay my bills? How am I going to survive?

Chloe forced me out as she wanted Charles for herself. I was furious. I was left without a job to pay my bills and survive in a country I had been successfully living in for eight years.

As I entered the elevator and pressed the ground floor, I could only think of calling my old boss, Sandra. Exiting the building and locating Sandra's number in my phone, I called immediately.

'Hello, Sandra.'

'Hey, Samantha! How are you? Long time no see.'

'Yes, it has been a while. I had been busy working, and yesterday, I had to leave work because my three-year visa ran out, and I was forced to resign temporarily. So, in all honesty, I am calling to ask if I could work for you again until I receive my documents back from the Home Office.'

'I could do with some help. However, the shop is not as busy as it used to be, so I can't pay you the £45 a day that I did in the past, I can give you £40, and if you do overtime, I will add an extra £10 for every hour. Would that be OK?'

Knowing that I had no other option, I accepted the offer. *It's better than nothing. I don't have anyone I can depend on, so this is it—for now,* I thought before reluctantly answering yes.

Three months had passed since I sent my application for an extension, and I had heard nothing back, not even a progress letter to inform me that my case had been allocated to a case worker—nothing. Being a realist, I took my faith into my own hands by emailing the admissions team at Warwick Business School and requesting a deferral by explaining my current situation. A few weeks later, I received a confirmation email informing me that my request had been accepted and I should be able to commence the course next year.

After five months, I was certain that being a hairstylist was not my calling. I was grateful that at least I had a job that covered my rent and a little left over to cover my food and travel, although most mornings, I walked from the flat where I resided (Lower Tulse Hill) to the shop (West Norwood). It was a good little trek, but I enjoyed it. My morning journey helped me to remain optimistic and present.

'Sam, you finished?' asked Sandra once more.

'Yeah, I'm coming', I replied reluctantly while returning my uneaten food to its carrier bag and placing it in the refrigerator.

'What would you like me to do?' I asked.

'Perm Nicki's hair.'

'OK, all of it?'

'Her hair is a nightmare. Just touch up around the edges. I'm going to do a ponytail and a wide fringe.'

'Right, so is this amount enough?' I asked while showing her the mixing bowl and the application brush.

'Nicki, can you please have a seat in this chair?'

'No problem. Pump up the chair a little higher. Thanks', said Nicki as I covered her with a protective fabric and then a towel.

'So, Sam, you used to work for Sandra a while back. What made you return?' asked Nicki.

'Honestly, Nicki, immigration woes', I replied with a deep, drawn-out sigh. 'I have been struggling, on my own, with my status for years now. Every year, for the last four, the immigration law has changed. Recently, I learnt that migrants will have to re-apply for an extension every two and a half years; for how long, I am unsure. But I believe you reapply five times. Just don't quote me on that. All I know is that I have had enough. I am tired! I had to stop my studies several times, and now it has impacted my work', I groaned.

'Believe you me, I too, more than anyone else, know what they put people through, especially people from the Caribbean—specifically Jamaicans. I have been dealing with this for over twenty-five years! On several occasions, they have tried to deport me, but I went for the most reputable immigration lawyers I can find to fight it.'

'They can't get rid of her!' interrupted Sandra, coupled with a cheesy grin.

'Damn right! I've lived here for too long. It's gonna take more than a deportation summons or a detention hold to get me out of the UK', said Nicki.

'That's true! I have been on many visits to Bedford Detention Centre, where you and my mom were held, and I have heard many stories of how you behaved for them not to deport you. You are definitely one of a kind', I concurred.

The conversation went to Nicki reminiscing about past transgressions and memories. I zoned in and out of the conversation until I completed delivering the service to Nicki. The entire process took a little under seventy minutes.

My final straw was not being able to finish eating my lunch or dinner. I was being worked like a modern-day slave—only allowed forty-five minutes to complete a full head of weave. This service typically takes anywhere from 60 to 120 minutes, but I only had forty-five minutes. My mind, body, and soul could not take a moment more of this. I had reached my peak.

*God, I don't want to come across as ungrateful because had it not been for Sandra, I would not have been able to work to cover my immediate bills, but I am tired to my core.* I pleaded with God in my head while wrapping Nicki's hair. After placing her under the hair dryer, I dragged my aching body, sore from head to toe, to a salon chair.

*This is the part that I hate. Why can't I just get my bloody money so that I can go home? I'm grateful today, but it is a little depressing. I would love to take today off, but I don't have that luxury. All I can afford to do is stare at people in resorts having the time of their lives—hoping and praying that my time is coming soon. I was here almost three hours before Sandra arrived at the shop, and now, I must wait until she feels like it before she pays me. Piss take!* I concluded as I pulled my phone out of my pocket.

Thirty minutes later, while playing with my phone, Sandra instructed me to check Nicki's hair.

'It dry?'

'About 95 per cent dry.'

Alright! Take her out and blow-dry her hair until it dries.'

'OK', I responded while switching the dryer off.

'So, what do you want me to do with her hair after?'

'Glue in five tracks at the front, then catch up the rest of her hair into a ponytail.'

'OK', I said as I started to section out Nicki's hair.

'Wait! Let me section the fringe. Hand me the glue and the tracks', commanded Sandra.

So I did.

'OK, continue following my pattern. Here is the comb.'

'In this direction?' I asked as I parted Nicki's hair diagonally.

'Yes, just like that.'

Eighteen minutes later, I confirmed with Sandra that I was finished.

'Great! Gel up the rest of her hair to the centre of her head', said Sandra.

'Like a high pony?'

'Yes, just like that. Then, wrap this around Nicki's head so her hair dries smoothly. Also, put these over her ears to protect them', Sandra directed.

After following Sandra's instructions, I returned Nicki to the hair dryer and turned the timer to forty minutes.

*I'm done now!* I thought as I eased into the chair I had Nicki in a few seconds ago.

'How long do you have left with her hair?' I asked Sandra who was applying the finishing touches on the customer sitting in her chair.

'She's done!' declared Sandra as she used a towel to remove the loose hair that fell on her shoulders when she removed the cape tied around her for protection.

'Amazing! It looks fabulous!' I directed the customer as she admired her pixie cut that enhanced her cheekbones in the mirror.

'Thank you! It's perfect. It is better than pictures in the hair magazine', said the customer as she thanked Sandra and handed some money to her.

Twenty-six minutes later, she took Nicki out from under the hair dryer. Checking her fringe, Sandra realised that there was still a little wait and directed me to use the hand dryer to speed up the process, so I did.

When Nicki's hair dried, I recoiled into the chair. I then returned to my phone and noticed a missed call with a corresponding voicemail. *I wonder who left a voice message on my phone?* After all, I had been feeling quite jittery all day.

'Something is coming; I can feel it', I murmured as I dialled my voicemail.

Good evening, Miss White, this is Karim, your solicitor. Sorry that I missed you. I've got great news, and I couldn't wait until Monday. YOU GOT IT!! Please come to my office Monday to collect your documents. Again, congratulations!' Mr Karim said before he ended the call.

I was shocked. I was shaking. To ensure that I heard Mr Karim's voice message correctly, I re-listened to the message, and then upon hearing him say congratulations, I screamed a second time. In a panic, I scrolled through my email, and there it was—the evidence.

RE: Your ILR Application

Hi Sam,

Your application for settlement has been granted. Please arrange a date for you to come and collect your documents.

Congratulations.

Regards,

Karim Michaels

'A wah? What happened?' Sandra and Nicki asked.

'I Got My Indefinite!' I blurted.

'Congratulations!', said Sandra.

'Wah? True? A Lie? Mek, mi see!' shouted Nicki as she tried to grab my phone out of my hand.

'Wait, wait! Let mi find it!' Locating the message, I showed her, and then she jumped out of her seat and started cheering.

'To be frank, I woke up this morning and felt different. It could be that I am a year older—it was my birthday last week, Saturday. And for the past nine years, I have been granted a Home Office status extension around my birthday. So, from the start of October, I have been looking for some form of a response from them. It is as if my case officer gets a sense of accomplishment from stamping my passport around my birthday. I had a feeling I would be granted my settlement on my birthday', I said.

'It was your birthday last week Saturday. Why didn't you say something?' asked Sandra.

'I didn't want to make a fuss, especially when I had nothing to be happy for', I confessed.

'What a birthday gift!' said Nicki.

'So, what happened? Did you contact Charles as he instructed and tell him the good news?' enquired Tracy.

'I did! I sent him a WhatsApp message the moment I stepped out of my solicitor's office the following Monday afternoon. He responded almost immediately. After a month of renegotiation, I went back to work at the media company. I learned that two people tried to do my role while I was off, and they both quit because I was performing two people's jobs in one.

'Despite them trying to draw me back to work under the guise that I knew the system better than the people they had employed, I went back because I wanted to save as much money as I could to put towards my study commencing the following October (2017).'

'And here you are! Sam, you must pat yourself on the shoulder. You have endured so much. I am proud of you. Keep it up, and you will get through this. I believe that you will', said Tracy while simultaneously hugging me.

'Thanks, Tracy, this means a lot—more than you will ever know.'

'Right, we must return to work. I looked at the milk cages earlier, and they are running low. Go into the cooler and restock the milk. After you complete that, look at the other juices and replenish those, if necessary. Once you have replenished the cooler stock, come and find me so I can instruct you on what to do', said Tracy.

'Will do. See you in a bit', I said as I exited the staff room.

Fall forward. Progress is a messy and complex process. Sometimes, you may need to be pulled or held back for God to reposition you onto the correct path for your purpose. Take note: you will fall several times, but remember to get up.

***Gratitude is necessary.***

Having a spirit of gratitude keeps you grateful and humble. Isaiah informs us that the Lord will make your goals happen in time, so do not worry about being held back. Identify the small things you are grateful for and let them remind you that the righteous will fall several times and rise again, but the wicked will stumble in calamities.

*"The smallest family will become a thousand people, and the tiniest group will become a mighty nation. At the right time, I, the Lord, will make it happen."*
Isaiah 60:22

# RE-ROUTE

'How far have you gotten, Sam?' asked Tracy. 'I have completed the milk and organic drinks section. I am about to finish merchandising these drinks, then I will work my way to the cheese aisle.'

'Stop just before the cheese aisle. I want you to replenish the large drinks aisle: water and large fizzy drinks.'

Rearranging the large water bottles, in my absent mind, one slipped from my grip and almost caused the entire cage to topple over. A patron passing by grabbed the cage and stabilised it long enough for me to jump off the mobilised ladder and remove the bottle that fell out of my hand.

*Phew!*

'Thank you so much!'

'No worries, just in the right place at the right time.'

'No, it could have been a disaster, so thank you!'

So many times, I was headed toward disaster, and it was averted.

## Second Act

***

'Hello?'

'Good morning. Am I speaking with Miss White, Samantha White?'

'Yes, you are. Who, may I ask, is calling?'

'Hi, this is Chloe from your previous employer, media company. So, I have been informed by Charles that you have received a settlement and that you are open to reinstating your old position. Is this true?'

'Yes, all of that is correct.'

'I have booked an appointment between yourself, Charles, and Pat on the 27th at 10:30 a.m. Would that be convenient?'

'Yes, that would be perfect.'

After a month of renegotiations, I went back to work at the media company and demanded a higher wage, and they had no other option but to concede.

Returning to the office felt strange. I left like a bad decision, hidden from everyone, and now I must explain why I left in the first place. The thought of walking into the office with my stuff that had not been removed from the box I brought it home in months ago weighed on me.

Bright and early Thursday morning, I got ready and headed to the office in central London. Arriving at 10:15 a.m., I was greeted by a familiar atmosphere. Approaching the reception, I saw a recognisable face before being directed to the third floor, where I was told to be seated until Charles came out of the office to meet me.

An unmistakable face greeted me as he exited the elevator. As Charles walked towards me, our eyes met, and we hugged. Inhaling his perfume, I nestled my head onto his arm. A few minutes later, he separated us while starting to distance himself from me, simultaneously looking into one of the transparent offices opposite where we were standing.

Intrigued, I followed his eyeline only to see him staring at Chloe, who was meeting with another individual in the room.

*Well, that explains his behaviour.*

She never took her eyes off us as we walked past the room. *Maybe they are dating. I will act accordingly.*

So, as we located the room, I reverted to my professional stance and focused on negotiating my wages and a date that I could start working, which we agreed would be the last week of November.

Thirty minutes later, all terms of my contract were met, so the meeting was terminated, and we exited the room. On our way to the elevator, Charles made an extra effort to display professionalism between us because Chloe was piercing a hole in the back of my head. So, to reassure her, he shook my hand just before I entered the elevator.

Returning to the office a week later, the atmosphere was the same, and I slid back into the role as if nothing had changed. Except it had.

Month-end had occurred, and with a massive backlog from several people quitting, I did not have the time to relax like the others. So, I kept my head down by starting early and ending late. Chloe was in our building almost every day and sometimes twice per day. I believe I had lunch with Charles on a couple occasions, yet I caught him looking at me many times, which made team meetings tense.

The tension between us was so overwhelming it followed me home many a night. After dreaming about him in uncompromisable positions, I decided to stay away from him in all circumstances. This unfortunately came to a head during our holiday party.

The second week of December had come around, and all staff members were excited about the office party. Everyone was buzzing, trying to come up with unique ideas within the confines of the company's theme: Disco. Not wanting to spend much money, I scoured the internet, where I found a dancing outfit—tutu, leg warmers, fluorescent bracelets, and headband. *This is my outfit.* So, my entire outfit was a black jumpsuit accessorised with a green tutu, ankle and wrist warmers, fluorescent bracelets, necklace, and headband—I looked like a fairy in the dark—my ultimate intention.

Some people made more effort than others. Specifically, Charles, who wore a fitted male jumpsuit with arms and wrapped around him, was a humungous fuchsia flamingo. He went over the top—the only manager to do so. Our energy matched.

Migrating to the venue was an experience. Some of us were lucky to grab a black cab with the head of Finance—I was one of the lucky ones—a first-time experience. The venue was smack bang in the city and looked like a makeshift building. Although there was an entrance door and bouncers, the interior had exposed bricks and some scaffolding. I was unsure whether the building was under construction or simply had a rustic décor. Moreover, it was under a train station, which aligned well with its overall aesthetics. *This must be the décor the owners were going for.*

After over twenty minutes in the drinks queue, I emerged from the bar and found some of my team on the dance floor, and of course, I joined them. "24K Magic", by Bruno Mars, was bellowing in the air, and everyone was dancing—some more so than others.

Looking for eye candies across the room, my eyes scanned Chloe, but I simply looked beyond her. Frankly,

I had been through too much this year to care anything about her.

I heard earlier in the month that she had dug her claws into Charles, and her decision to remove me in May was all a ploy to eliminate her competition so she could have him all to herself. What she didn't know was I saw him first; we were attracted to each other the moment we laid eyes on each other. In short, if I wanted him, I could have him whether I was employed there or not. He gave me his number for a reason, but I wasn't interested.

Throughout the night, we were on and off the dance floor. I glimpsed Charles doing the same. Sometimes, he stayed with Chloe to reassure her as it was apparent that she could not hold a beat.

Have I forgiven her? In all honesty, yes, but I will never forget. Avoidance is the only solution to keep my focus.

The DJ dropped "Dancing on My Own" by Calum Scott, and the crowd went wild. Charles deflated his flamingo so that he could snuggle up to Chloe. Most people danced with someone, and those who did not have that special someone—like myself—danced in groups with team members and other distant colleagues. This song was repeated twice, and at the end of it, I went to search for food.

'I am starving! Did you see where we could get something to eat? Finger food, for example?' asked Jemma.

'I believe I saw a sign that says "Food Queue" in neon lights in the bar where we were queuing for drinks. We need to go there and check.'

So, we left the dance floor and headed to find food.

I spent over thirty minutes waiting in line to select something to eat. It was our time to choose. We went for hamburgers and potato fries, the most filling meal on the menu. We found a little nook where we were able to balance and eat, as there was nowhere to do so. After chomping down our meals in no time, "Work" by Rhianna woke up the entire venue.

The building was in a frenzy. Most people were heading to the dance floor. It was jam-packed. Returning to the music hall was a nightmare, but Jemma and I clung to each other to not get misplaced as we forced our way to the initial location where our other team members congregated. By the time we managed to get there, the DJ had repeated the song.

'Yes, yes!' I screamed.

Leaning on the wall, I danced by myself and then with my team. While we were dancing as a team, my friend Sarah whispered, 'Charles is on the dance floor. He is two persons away from you.'

Rolling my eyes, I said, 'I don't care! He is with Chloe now.'

'But it's obvious that he's attracted to you. Dance with him. It's just a dance!' persisted Sarah while we simultaneously threw our hands up in the air as we swayed to the music. It was so obvious that Sarah wanted to live vicariously through me.

With her boost and the atmosphere's energy, I started dancing a little freer. Suddenly, Sarah stared past me and pointed while mouthing that Charles was immediately behind me. His back was touching mine. A bag of emotions, I started to slow down my movements. My heart was in my mouth.

I heard a whisper. *Don't be shy now, Sam; it's just an innocent dance between two colleagues on the dance floor.*

Feeling a little more confident, I turned around and started to move with less inhibition. Charles then turned to face me. The room became empty, and only he and I were on the dance floor. The attraction between us at the start of May was resurrected. The same feeling came over me when he backed me up against the pillar by his desk in the office. Although surrounded by a room of people, I only saw him. He leaned over to say something to me, but all I saw were his lips moving.

Then it happened!

'Sam, it's time to take your break', said Fatima.

'This is my last break, right?' I asked her.

'I believe so, but I will check the rota.'

So, while I was waiting, I rolled the remaining bags of bottled water and fizzy drinks back into the warehouse and carefully positioned the cages back into their slot.

'Yes, this is your final break. After this, you have the bakery to clean', said Fatima.

Humans are cardinal beings and usually make decisions based on the easy route and the actions that generate the fastest gratification. You could make short-term decisions that change the entire trajectory of your life, so be sober-minded and try to make decisions after you have performed a substantial level of research.

**Key**: If you try to skip a process, you might be redirected, especially if there is a necessary step that you need to go through.

***Trust the process.***

You will be re-routed if you try to skip a stage of your journey. With every challenge or trial you face and overcome, you would have obtained a skill. Jonah tried to skip out on his duty, and God redirected his path. This skill is needed to fight the next challenge, and you will not be able to progress until you have obtained the skill.

---

*"...And the Lord appointed a great fish to swallow up Jonah, and Jonah was in the belly of the fish three days and three nights." Jonah 1:17*

---

# AUDACITY OF FAITH

'How far have you gotten, Sam?' asked Tracy. 'I have completed the pastry display panel. I am about to finish washing down the oven, then I will work my way to the fridge.'

'Hey, Sam. I was not very productive', said Charlotte.

'Leave the fridge for Charlotte. She is about to finish the cheese and meat aisle, so I'll give her that to complete', said Tracy.

'Thanks for the advice earlier, Sam. It was exactly what I needed to hear', said Charlotte.

'I'm glad I could help. We all must overcome challenges. The gift is the lesson you learn in overcoming; that's where you will obtain your greatest treasure! I know too well how it feels when your heart is set on something, then obstacles get in your way to distract you and steal your future.'

'Thank you again! How do you know so much?' enquired Charlotte.

'I have experienced some world-shattering challenges, and I was only able to move on by searching for the lessons embedded in each of them. Unfortunately, if you don't retrieve the gems, life will deliver the same challenges in different scenarios until you have learnt the lessons. Believe me, I know.'

## Blind Faith
### ***

Chaos ensued after that December night during the office holiday party. Feelings were hurt, and I decided to leave early. Weeks passed, and working in that environment became quite unbearable. With no indication of my contract being extended after December, I started applying for roles elsewhere. Upon securing a position, I informed Charles, Pat, and Gary that I would be leaving in January 2017 because they were dragging their feet. After being released in May 2016, I promised myself I would never leave my future in anybody's hands again.

On the 10th of February 2017, I bid goodbye to the media company. This transition felt right. I was not leaving in the late night after everyone went home. An hour before most people would be organising to leave the office, the finance team all congregated around me. Charles gave a speech, and a few more managers gave well wishes. A few hugs and well wishes were exchanged. I was gifted with chocolate and a bottle of wine.

Bright and early Monday morning, the 13th of February, I commenced a new role at a retail organisation. Migrating to a new organisation and role, one thing was a constant: me. *Now was the opportunity to reinvent myself.* However, everywhere I go, there I am. My perception and values were challenged on all levels.

Being the only Black employee in this organisation made me feel quite uncomfortable. Every day felt like a fight. My back was against the wall, but I am no quitter, so with that knowledge in my arsenal, I knew I had to become a chameleon. I learnt how to code-switch as many of the employees spoke with an upper-class accent, and I learnt quite early that people would not give you the floor or listen to you unless you sounded like them.

God's grace protected me with the provision of my manager, Paul Myers. He was kind, helpful, and patient. He was a great teacher, and I wanted to learn as much as I could to increase my employability. My strategy was to turn up thirty minutes early every day, and I did my job with no complaints, although sometimes they were warranted. Also, I spoke less and listened more, which made blending in a smoother transition.

Months of contorting myself into a pretzel made me ill. Sunday nights were the most painful because I knew I had to transform into someone my spirit did not recognise. I hated it. My appetite diminished, and my hair fell out. I recoiled into myself, and every minute I spent at work dragged me further into depression. My light at the end of this dark tunnel was knowing I would return to university in September, but it was taking too long.

To stay positive, I went for walks during my lunch hour. Remaining focused was paramount, so I started fasting in July because although I knew that I would commence my course, I did not know how I was going to pay for it. So, I did the thing that I knew had never failed me—*I fasted.*

The answer I sought from God was delivered on the last day of my church's convocation —28th of August 2017. It was provided by Bishop Rogers, the last hour on the last day. I was convicted. This was the answer that I had been waiting on.

A month had passed since the preacher at my church's annual convocation pointed me out in the congregation and instructed me to "...go to university. God says everything will be alright..."

Knowing that this was two years coming and that I had been fasting for over a month, this confirmation was what I'd been fasting and praying for. So, with no hesitation, I handed in my resignation to Charles. It was not too difficult to part ways, as most people knew from February 2016, when I received confirmation from both universities that I would return to school to obtain my master's. Once you know your purpose, you "...must be about your father's business..." a phrase that I have heard too frequently and that has been my compass and north star.

For many weeks, even before I received confirmation to walk by faith and re-register back in the master's program, I had been searching for ways to raise the finances that I needed to cover the tuition fee, accommodation, and the cost of council tax on my council flat in London, as the ability to obtain a loan for my programme was not readily available.

One late Saturday, after weeks of scouring the internet, I stumbled upon a company that proposed a conditional offer to obtain a loan pending documents and evidence review. Having no other option, I accepted its terms.

I got my cousin to move into my studio flat during this time. Also, he had verbally agreed to cover the rent while I paid for the council tax. So, knowing that I would not lose my flat while studying for my master's in the Midlands, I could focus on working hard to achieve the best grade possible.

After reading the message that my application for the loan was declined, I panicked for a few minutes. Even though I did not know what outcome would be revealed, I knew it would work out for my good. So, with that, I was resolute; I would not turn back. Anything is better than what I just left; after all, God, you told me "...to go to university, it will work out for my good..." so I am handing my worries to you.

Arriving at my accommodation, it was late at night, and after unpacking my stuff and thanking O'Shane, I collapsed into bed.

The next day, I woke up after 10:00 a.m. and missed my housemate.

After rummaging around my bags, I stumbled upon some CVs I had printed out a few weeks before I resigned. *Well, I need a job or two if I am going to do this.* So, after having some breakfast, I spent the next three hours scanning the internet to locate recruitment agencies to apply for part-time jobs that would provide flexibility.

Unsatisfied with my progress, I searched for the university's address and used the instructions to get there. Two more hours of enquiring about job availabilities with all the stores located on the campus, with no luck. So, with nothing to lose, I got ready and headed out to Coventry Town Centre. Then, later, I went to the university's campus to try my luck. Walking into Rootes Grocery, I enquired there. However, earlier that morning, I contacted the recruitment agency that supplied them with employees, and they reassured me that no shifts were available. As faith would have had it, I secured one shift.

With over £7,000 in tuition fees plus £300 per month for rent and all costs for food and travel plus the council tax for my flat in London, I did not know how I would cover all those expenses. All I could do was focus on the present and showcase my diligence and dedication. I hope this will increase favour so that I can gain extra shifts. *That's what I will do.*

In October, I had to secure a second job as a cleaner at Coventry University Hospital. This was not ideal, but being unable to cover my debt, I had no choice. I had too much skin in the game—I gave up everything in London based on God's instruction. Yes, all I have is blind faith and favour.

A few weeks had passed since I sat my Strategy and Analysis Exam, and honestly, I am not sure how I performed. With only a little over four hours of sleep each day, I had been operating on empty with extra caffeine and sugar since I started this journey.

One late Thursday night at the end of November, I received my Strategy Analysis and Practice grade, stating that I had failed my exam. Devastated, I gave everything I had to my exam; the result shook me to my core. I was so numb and in shock. I thought I would have passed at least with a low grade as I hadn't much time to thoroughly prepare due to work, but to have failed. I was so disappointed with myself and my situation. What is extremely frustrating is that I knew that I could do better, but my situation limited how much effort I could give. It was *not fair.*

I was the only person on my course of almost one hundred people who worked. I was working so hard, the hardest I have ever worked in my entire life, just to pay tuition and sit in a class that I failed. *What am I going to do? It is true when they say that poverty is a sin*', I reflected before sobbing all the way to my accommodation.

"Good evening, customers. You have fifteen minutes before the store closes; please gather your groceries and make your way to the cashier", announced Tina over the speaker.

'Wow! It's time already', I said, surprised.

'Yes, it is and not too soon. Let's face up, make sure the store looks presentable for tomorrow', said Tracy.

Exhausted from working the graveyard shift since Friday, there was no way I would be cooped up in a student chair. *I need a bed to rest my head tonight.* With this as my focus, I asked around the store until I secured a local cab, which I ordered ten minutes before closing.

Two minutes before closing, I received confirmation that the cab was outside.

After saying goodnight to everyone, I was off, seated securely in the back seat of the cab with my rucksack and all other stuff.

Life is a journey. Like a heartbeat, all 'living'/active processes have a rhythm that increases and decreases.

Joshua reminds us to be courageous and not discouraged because every process you go through is establishing you. You are perfectly and wonderfully made; you do not need to alter your existence to fit society's perception of you. Focus on being the best version of yourself. You have treasures in you that no one else can fulfil.

***Be fixed on purpose and flexible on route to achieve it.***

Being open to travelling a path not frequently visited may be necessary to help you accomplish your goal. Hold steadfast to your purpose, but be open to utilising different mediums to help you achieve it.

---

*"Be strong and courageous. Do not be afraid; do not be discouraged, for the Lord your God will be with you wherever you go." Joshua 1:9*

---

# HOPE REMAINS

· · · · · · · · · · · · · · · · · · ◆ · · ◆ · · · · · · · · · · · · · · · · · · ·

S o, here I am, over two years later, sprinting barefooted along a grassed lawn in the middle of July with the sun challenging and cheering me on simultaneously in a cloudless sky.

One foot after the other, I pound the path.

*I will be on time if it kills me. I've worked too hard. I will not miss my moment.*

Falling on my face will not stop me. Not making eye contact, I jump up, brush myself off, and continue, checking directions along the path.

Bursting through the gymnasium's double doors is mesmerising. The building is a maze, cordoned off with beautifully decorated temporary pop-up shops from the registration point, photobooths room, and robe collection room to ensure COVID regulations are upheld.

'Hello! Can I still collect my gown? I ask.

'Can I see your wristband?'

'Here you go!'

'Thanks. Have a seat.'

As I sit, awaiting my gown and sash, I reflect on the last two years. It has been an emotional rollercoaster. There have been times when I thought that I would not make it.

*Thank you, Lord!* I reflect as salty water hits my lips...

## Breaking Point
### ***

zzzzzZZZZZZ!!

The phone's vibration on the wooden nightstand jolted me out of sleep. Frantically scrummaging around for it, I found it lodged between the nightstand and bed. It must have fallen off from the vibration.

With a throbbing headache, I checked the time before I scanned my email for a response: nothing.

With it being 05:47 a.m., I put the phone on snooze until 06:00 a.m. before jumping into the shower.

Barely making it in for my first lesson at 09:00 a.m., my body carried the memories of the past three days and two nights of working and sleeping on campus. I ached from head to toe, desperate for a long, relaxing bath.

Two hours had passed, and I was becoming uneasy. Focusing was becoming an idea my mind was struggling to grasp as I faced off with a new assignment. Coupled with other commitments and the weekly Credit Control reminders, I was drowning. My grip on reality was waning, slowly tipping my perception of it. With that said, I was overwhelmed.

Heart racing, head aching with sharp pains shooting up from the base of my neck; I was suffocating. *Let me grab my asthma pump.*

Waking up in the doctor's office hours later, I was ordered to lie with a nebuliser for thirty minutes. This was the rude awakening I needed to step off this conveyor belt of destruction. Checking my phone as I exited the doctor's office approximately thirty-six minutes later, I scrolled over my email, and there it was.

'Thank you, Lord!' I shouted.

I was floating—the weight of the circumstance evaporated.

After laying in the doctor's office in the centre of campus for over an hour, I had my blood pressure checked and a bacon, lettuce, and tomato (BLT) sandwich to eat; I was given consent to go home.

En route to my accommodation, I rang the supermarket and explained what had transpired earlier. I confirmed that I was instructed to take the rest of the day off by the attending general practitioner (GP) who assisted me. Reassuring them that I would be back by Friday to work over the weekend, I thanked them for giving me the next few days off on sick leave, and then we ended the conversation. Returning to my accommodation, I melted into the fabric of the bed. I was out cold.

"Bum, bum, bum. Sam, Sammy, are you there?" enquired my housemate.

Opening my eyes, my head was throbbing.

'Yes', I screeched, followed by a slow, painful moan.

'How are you?' I saw that you left your rucksack in the kitchen. It has been there since yesterday.'

'Yesterday? Is today the 5th of December?' I asked as I shuffled to a seating position. 'I slept for an entire day?!' I said in shock, rubbing my forehead.

'Yes, today is the 5th of December. It seems like it. You have been burning the midnight oil at both ends. You appear to be burnt out.'

'Definitely! I had a panic attack Monday at the end of my first class', I said.

'What? Really? How did you get home?'

'I felt my chest tightening up, and while rummaging in my bag for my asthma pump, I believe I passed out because I woke up in the GP's surgery. I was put on a nebuliser for thirty minutes. After that, I was instructed by the doctor to go home. Also, I applied for my degree to be deferred. I am exhausted!

'I need to raise £6,000 to cover the rest of my tuition fee. To do so, I must get a full-time job because working and studying is draining me.'

'OK! So, how is that going? Have you received an answer?' Shauna asked with a bit of uncertainty.

'Yes, I received confirmation yesterday. So, I will spend the next few days applying to as many contract roles as possible.'

'Oh, that's good. Do you still work at the supermarket on campus?'

'Yes, I do. I'm going to see whether I can get some overtime while I work on securing other roles. I need to save up to pay off my tuition fee. Ideally, I'd like to obtain my citizenship too. But I will wait and see. By the way, do you have any painkillers? My head feels like I was being hit in the head.'

'I believe so; let me look', said Shauna as she left my room.

A few seconds later, she gave me two, explaining that I should get something to eat before I took them. So, I scurried downstairs and boiled an easy-cook sachet of noodles in the microwave.

Once cooled, I devoured them and even drank the water. 'Shoot, I was hungry!' I said in disbelief before I took the tablets and went back to bed.

Waking up Wednesday afternoon, I was exhausted. The more I slept, the worse I felt. So, I made the bed, had a shower, and went for a walk. With no urgency, I let the wind direct me and walked to a superstore supermarket along a path I had never travelled. Twenty minutes later, I was manoeuvring through some bushes before coming to a canal.

*I am tired! I should end it here. I'm tired of fighting and getting nowhere, seeing no progress. Everyone passing me by.*

Falling on my knees, I screamed into the arm of my jacket. I screamed the hardest I could. Walking away minutes later with an even worse headache than I started with, I started reasoning with God to get some sense of direction.

Returning to my accommodation, I was feeling focused and motivated. I sat on the bed and started applying for contract work. I applied to jobs that offered a minimum of a six-month contract so that I could save money for the course's tuition fee—back-to-back—only stopping to grab a bite to eat. Then I returned to it, finally stopping minutes to midnight before collapsing onto the bed.

Tossing and turning all night, this feeling of helplessness and frustration consumed me. I dreamt I was at the canal I stumbled upon earlier that day when the desire to end it all rose inside me. The desire to walk into it consumed me. *I am emotionally and physically drained, fighting with every fibre of my being to get this opportunity to study at this prestigious establishment.* I need it to end. I saw myself as Ophelia in Sir Millais' painting. I embodied the image, and I gave in. As I stepped out to walk into the canal, I was jolted out of my dream with a phone call.

The desire still lingered, and I was convicted to end my life.

Checking the time, it was 04:30 a.m., 8th of December. It was Pastor Trevor. I revealed my dream to him. Immediately, he started to pray for me, and approximately five hours later, he finished, and just like the overwhelming desire that I had to end my life subsided.

Afterwards, I thanked him and then organised the room. I had a new perspective. My degree was deferred. *This was my opportunity to refocus.*

My day was filled with phone calls, and later in the day, I received a call for an interview in Birmingham the following week.

Friday afternoon, I started my shift at the supermarket early and had the opportunity to speak with Michael, the store manager. I explained my situation to him and asked if there were any extra shifts I could pick up to start saving towards my debt. He agreed.

However, weeks passed, and I was no closer to securing a new job. I had been interviewing everywhere with no luck. All the potential employers needed a full-time employee—I required a fixed-term contract. While awaiting this, I also started doing overtime at the hospital as a cleaner.

Relentless, I could not give up. I needed to secure a role. I revisited my CV and analysed my experiences: Retail, Billings Analyst, Credit Controller... *There must be a role out there that I can secure from one of my many experiences.* With this in mind, I separated my 'working CV' into different job specifications. I applied for some more roles, and almost a month later, in late January, I was short-listed for a credit controller role at Coventry University located in the centre of Coventry.

The day arrived, and after over fifty minutes of intense conversation, I left the interview satisfied that I did the best I could in answering the questions. However, through my over-critical perspective, I believed I could have done better when answering a few of the questions.

On my way back to my accommodation, I released any regrets about the interview. I let go and let God have his way. *Whatever happens, Lord, I have faith that you know what's best for me.*

While waiting, I continued to apply for as many roles as I could. Also, I continued to work as a temporary cleaner at Coventry Hospital. Unsure if I had secured the credit controller position, I continued applying for more jobs in my spare time with no luck. Despite the many rejections, I remained optimistic and continued applying.

One Thursday afternoon, on my break, I met with Tracy, who informed me of a temporary position in the bar on campus. I told her I could work three days (Wednesday, Thursday, and Friday) after my shift at the supermarket.

While focusing on managing my time and trying to be as effective as possible, Becky noticed I was working more than usual. In a one-to-one conversation, I informed her that I deferred my studies because I needed to raise some funds to pay the remainder of my tuition fees. I left it there and continued with my work.

The following Friday, a vivacious lady popped into the supermarket and asked me to come to the bookstore to talk with her. Not overthinking it, I arrived early the following morning. She talked me through how the business operated, the role, and its specific duties.

'What do you think? Can you handle the responsibilities?' asked Jane.

'Yes, it seems straightforward enough. Sorry, why are you asking me?'

'Becky informed me that you were looking for a part-time role to help save up towards paying your tuition fees. Is that correct?'

'Yes, that is true, but Becky didn't inform me she was doing this.'

'She wanted to surprise you, I guess. So, do you want the role or not?'

'Oh, I do, thanks!' I blurted with a cheesy grin. 'So, what do I do now?'

'Bring your passport and P45 tomorrow, and I will scan and email *Unitemps* your information so they can update our database', said Jane.

'Oh, my goodness! Thank you so much! When am I expected to work?'

'Saturday and Sunday mornings. There is one extra thing that you will need to do: open and close the store. The university security holds the keys down the hill, a few metres from the Warwick Business School. Would this be a problem?'

'No, not at all. So, who will I be working with?'

'There are a few other staff members. You may need to supervise them for the time being while working here. Would that be an issue for you?'

'No, it should be fine. I have supervised before.'

'Brilliant! See you tomorrow with your documents, and I will try my best to get you on our books by next Friday at the latest. Right, I have got to go. See you tomorrow at 10:45 a.m. sharp.'

'Thank you so much. I will be here at 10:45 a.m. sharp.'


A week and a half later, on my way home from work, I checked my email and discovered that I had secured the role.

I fell on my knees and thanked the Lord. Within one month, I had secured five jobs. How was I going to manage? I did not know; only the grace of God would carry me through this phase of my life. After all, faith without works is dead.

Bright and early Monday morning, I strolled up to the building's reception, where I would be working. "Good morning, I am the new Credit Controller; my name is Samantha—'

'Ms White! Please walk over to the next table to get your hat.'

'OK,' I said, a little dazed from jolting out of my memory.

Exiting the gymnasium, I breathe a deep sigh of relief. There were so many times I wanted to let go and give up, but something inside of me would not allow me to give in.

Walking with my relatives towards the temporary marquee in the sweltering heat, I was floating on clouds.

*Well done, Sam! I am so proud of you.*

'Before you go to your seat, let's take pictures to celebrate your achievements. When you left London over two years ago, you only had £3,000 to your name and an ILR (Indefinite Leave to Remain); now you will be returning a British citizen and a master's graduate', said a family friend.

*You know what? I have accomplished a great deal. The knowledge I gained while obtaining this degree equates to much more.*

Can faith be realised without audacity? Audacity is bold risks. Taking bold risks is necessary to fulfil your purpose. Without faith, it is impossible to please God, and along your journey to accomplishing your goal, you will be tested. Take heed. The greater your test, the greater your impact. Trust the process.

The challenges that you find yourself in throughout your life arise to shape you into the person you need to become to accomplish your purpose. You need those challenges and trials; they are necessary to mould you to achieve all your dreams and goals.

**Faith equals audacity.**

Audacity is bold risk. Faith will require you to make decisions beyond the ordinary that could appear risky. Jeremiah reminds us that God has plans to prosper us, so be sober-minded. Do not make decisions from a place of envy, greed, competition, or jealousy. What is for you is for you, and no one can take it from you. Believe, stay focused, and stay humble. Run your race and remain grateful.

"For I know the plans I have for you, declares the Lord, plans to prosper you and not to harm you, plans to give you hope and a future." Jeremiah 29:11

# EPILOGUE

*"When troubles of any kind come your way, consider it an opportunity for great joy. Because you know that the testing of your faith produces perseverance."*
*James 1:2-3*

# EPILOGUE

One of the most challenging decisions of my life was cutting off my *Plan B*. In the past, I talked myself out of situations where I could not see a clear ending. I have learnt that if things are constant, no progress is being made: change is the only constant in life.

Deliberately preventing myself from jumping ship when situations get hard was one of my missions at this juncture. But in life, uncertainty is a surety garnished with sprinklings of challenges with every progress.

I would like to thank my family for their motivation when I felt like I was on the brink of throwing in the towel. Thank you to Aunty Lorraine for scraping me off my accommodation's floor by speaking life into me when I felt like my world was imploding and I was one decision away and wanted to give up. My big brother, Fenton, has been my confidant in my time of need. Lastly, this book is dedicated to the loving memory of Rose Farquharson, my selfless grandmother, who instilled in me a spirit of excellence and completeness that I aspire to daily.

*"For we walked by faith, not by sight."*
*2 Corinthians 5:7*

# ABOUT THE AUTHOR

SAMANTHA N. WHITE, MSc, TEFL, BSc (Hons)

S amantha N. White is a perpetually optimistic change agent and solutions advocate who prides herself in solving problems as they arise in her life. Her passion for problem-solving was ignited as a child growing up in Jamaica with her grandmother, who frequently left her in charge of running her convenience store. This fortitude has been solidified throughout her many challenges, which she uses to help people she encounters tackle the most challenging processes in their lives.

Migrating to the UK, Samantha endured eighteen years of disappointment and setbacks. Ten of those years were outlined in her previous book—How I Forced Pandora's

Box Shut – 7 Life-Shaking Events That Almost Broke Me. During that time, she remained steadfast in achieving her goals: Bachelor (Hon.) in Management Studies, Dual-TEFL qualifications, volunteer English and Mathematics teacher and a Master's in Business Consulting from Warwick University.

Through therapy and counselling, Samantha has learned to use her experience to inspire and galvanise those who have undergone and are still enduring setbacks through the utilisation of tools to overcome them through her books and advocacy.

You can continue following and learning more about Samantha White by visiting her website at www.samanthanwhite.com and SamanthaNWhite (SNW) on Instagram.